THE ART OF
PROGRAMMING WITH
VISUAL BASIC

Mark *Warhol*

WILEY

JOHN WILEY & SONS, INC.

New York • Chichester • Brisbane • Toronto • Singapore

Publisher: Katherine Schowalter
Editor: Tim Ryan
Managing Editor: Robert S. Aronds
Text Design & Composition: Pronto Design & Production Inc.
Illustrations: Michael Tkach

Designations used by companies to distinguish their products are often claimed as trademarks. In all instances where John Wiley & Sons, Inc. is aware of a claim, the product names appear in initial capital or all capital letters. Readers, however, should contact the appropriate companies for more complete information regarding trademarks and registration.

This text is printed on acid-free paper.

This publication is designed to provide accurate and authoritative information in regard to the subject matter covered. It is sold with the understanding that the publisher is not engaged in rendering legal, accounting, or other professional service. If legal advice or other expert assistance is required, the services of a competent professional person should be sought.

Library of Congress Cataloging-in-Publication Data:
Warhol, Mark.
  The art of programming with Visual Basic / Mark Warhol.
         p. cm.
  Includes index.
  ISBN 0-471-12853-8 (pbk. : alk. paper)
     1. BASIC (Computer program language) 2. Microsoft Visual BASIC.
I. Title.
QA76.73.B3W368   1995   95-32002
005.13'3—dc20   CIP

Printed in the United States of America
10 9 8 7 6 5 4 3 2 1

Acknowledgments

I wish to thank Michael Tkach for his efforts in providing the illustrations for this book, and for enduring many of my inane drawings and design sessions.

Dedicated to the memory of David, the man I met in the PATH station, who died because nobody listened and nobody cared.

The whole world changes. Every single time.

Contents *Contents*

THE ART OF PROGRAMMING WITH VISUAL BASIC
Mark Warhol

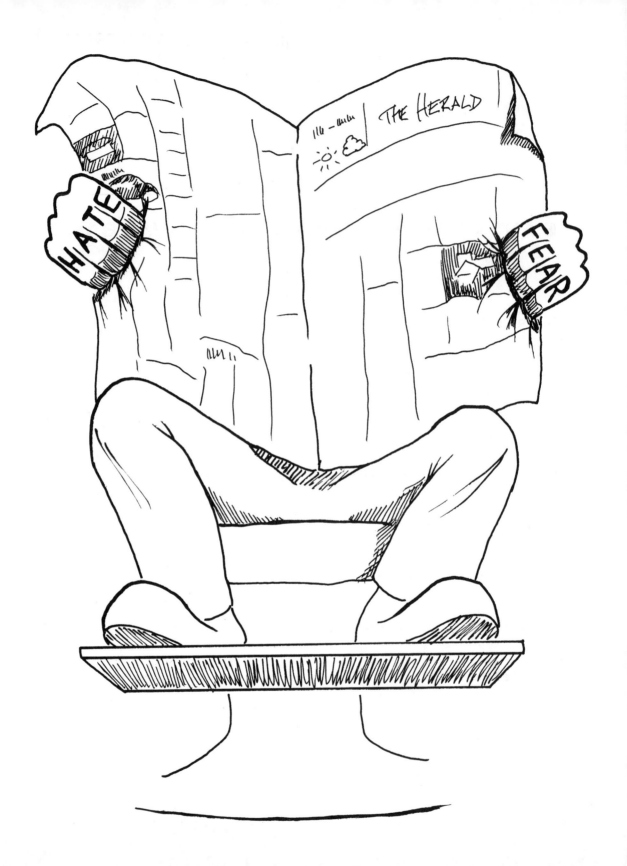

INTRODUCTION

When I was a little kid, I used to get a haircut at an old-fashioned barber shop. It was one of those places with a striped pole, ancient haircut pictures, and a collection of combs soaking in a half-filled jar of blue water. When he was finished cutting your hair, the barber showed you the back of your head in a big hand mirror. One of the barbers was really lousy and everybody always hoped they'd get the other guy.

One day when I was sitting in the barber chair getting my ears lowered, I looked down and saw a man waiting for a cut. He was reading a newspaper, and all I could see of him were two enormous hands, covered with coarse red hair. He had a letter tattooed on each of his knuckles. One hand spelled out HATE, the other FEAR. When you look into the mirrors that line the walls of an old-time barber shop, the reflections bounce back and forth, endlessly duplicating the image. All I could see stretched out to an infinite horizon was HATE and FEAR. HATE and FEAR. HATE and FEAR.

I didn't understand the significance of that image until I started developing in-house corporate applications. Now I relive that moment almost every single day. This is the story of my journey through the hate and fear, the pain and agony, and the torture and occasional triumph of real-world programming.

Before we begin, I might as well introduce myself. First of all, I am not a professional writer. My last book-writing endeavor was in the third grade. It was *Super Guppy*, the tale of a man-eating fish in the local pond. I'm not a programming genius, a guru, a technical evangelist, or any such nonsense. I'm not in cahoots with Microsoft or any special interest group. There are no lackeys feeding me secret info or rewriting my code. What I am is a real live Visual Basic (VB) programmer. I work as part of a team that develops both small and immeasurably large in-house applications using Visual Basic as a front end to communicate with an SQL Server. These are corporate applications developed for various user groups and functions. Development is structured around the applications life cycle paradigm. For the most part, all that this really means is that women try to avoid me in the halls.

A friend of mine who works as a Novell Netware engineer was looking for a career change and was thinking of getting involved in Windows programming. As a rather bizarre act of helpfulness, I decided to write down everything I felt was important about developing Visual Basic applications based on my experience. What resulted was a programmer's rant: an unformatted, single-spaced, 17-page stream of consciousness written in brutally short, cipher-like chapters. I shipped the whole mess off to her and tentatively gave it to a few people in my development staff. Their reviews were surprisingly favorable considering my third-grade fiasco. John Wiley & Sons, Inc. thought it had potential as a longer work.

However, this is not *The Complete Unabridged VB Power Bible for Idiots*. There are excellent and exhaustive books on VB, SQL, the SDK, API calls, graphics programming, and so on that can and should be read as part of your professional training. You don't need another book explaining 500 API calls. I already have two of them. This book is an attempt to fill in the cracks left by the other manuals. It is what I, a downtrodden, overworked programmer, feel is important for the success of an application. It represents about four years of my life spent screaming at the monitor wondering how I ever got into this mess in the first place.

This book has the same purpose as it did at 17 pages. It's one programmer's attempt to help save other developers some grief. Every topic, mundane or otherwise, is dealt with, because at some point I've seen it neglected or forgotten, and projects have suffered. Every war story is true. Everything I have to say is based on my experience in an actual development environment. This is not academic musings dreamed up while sipping an amaretto in a paneled den. I don't write computer programs for fun. I write them for a living. This book is everything that I know and do to survive a real application development project. This is the book I tried to read but couldn't find when I got out of computer school. It is in this spirit that I offer you this, my bizarre act of helpfulness.

May your pain be less than mine.

Product Disclaimer *Disclaimer*

All the following techniques, suggestions, admonishments, and condemnations are tainted by my own personal prejudices and experience. Each application development environment is different. Examine the appropriateness of the ideas to your current situation. Test out everything I say. Remember that as VB and Windows both change, all the code techniques I show will eventually become dated and perish. I hope the concepts behind them will not.

The text assumes you already have a working knowledge of Visual Basic, SQL, and standard programming logic structures. I am using constants from the file CONSTANT.TXT wherever possible instead of hardcodes.

WHAT'S IN A NAME?

The Structure of My Argument: I've Got Just One Thing to Say

The biggest problem with Visual Basic is that it's easy to get started. Once it's installed, you can begin creating forms, adding controls, and writing code snippets based on the fractured examples in the manual. Then you can save your project as PROJECT1.MAK in the Visual Basic directory. You have a nice little form called FORM1.FRM that is filled with controls like **Command1**, **Text1**, and **Checkbox1**. Now you can make an executable file, bundle it up with VBRUN300.DLL, and you've written an application.

As far as I can tell, this is what every manual I've read seems to be doing. No standards, no naming conventions, no common global routines. Every function is written at the form level because I guess it's more fun that way. I develop Visual Basic applications for a living, so I can tell you that developing like this is not fun. It is suicidal.

There is only one idea I really want to get across in this book. You can learn all the API calls, DLLs, and cool little coding secrets from a dozen other places. But if you do not adhere to consistent standards in your application setup, naming conventions, form design and coding, you're going to have an unmanageable application that will be a maintenance disaster. All the fancy coding tricks and all those jazzy 3-D controls and all those APIs aren't going to save you. You'll just be painting a clown's face on a dead man.

Let's just start with an example to set the mood.

A form has a command button that is named **Command1**. What does this mean? It doesn't mean anything. Not now, and not six months from now when you're going through the application someone in your development group wrote just before he or she left for another job. A hundred lines into a subroutine you see this statement:

```
Call Command1_Click
```

Now you have to go find the **Command1** control and see what it's actually supposed to do. Does it save data? Maybe it exits the form. All you know is that it's 4:45 P.M. on a Friday and you have to get this program up and running for a demo on Monday morning at 8:00. The form is filled with controls defaulted to the vanilla VB naming convention. This subroutine references global variables. They have names like **dw** and **ky** and **sss**. There is a global variable called **emp_id.** There is a form level variable called **emp_id.** There is a local variable called **emp_id.** Which one of these is the subroutine really trying to assign? A variable passed by reference into this subroutine is being assigned a value accidentally, but you don't realize it because its name is **x** and you thought it was a local variable.

The programmer has written yet another weird variation of a numeric check in the keypress event of a field. Menu items don't correspond to locations in any other application. The form has a weird background color and some of the fields are in Courier font, others in Times Roman. There is no way to determine from this routine's name whether it's a subroutine or a function. But there is a really cool API call that makes the cursor switch to a lightning bolt when it's passed over certain controls.

This can be your reality. It is not fun. But it is now 5:45 P.M. on a Friday and you're not going anywhere.

Are you frightened? Good. Let's start looking at what we will need to do to prevent this situation from happening to you. Our goal is pretty basic.

What Do We Want?

Consistency.

Where do we want it?
1. In naming conventions.
2. In presentation (GUI design).

3. In program operation (global routines, standard coding practices).

Why?
1. Consistency in presentation and operation results in user confidence in the system.
2. Consistency in naming conventions and programming practices results in clear and easily maintained code.

How are we going to do this?

By adopting standards that will help ensure consistency.

The next section deals with naming conventions, one of the most crucial and neglected aspects of a successful programming project.

Command 1: Naming Objects

A standard prefix should be used when naming a form and all its objects. Visual Basic displays a fine list of prefixes on page 35 of *Programmer's Guide for VB 3.0*. I just found this out. You'd never know they had such a scheme if you look at all the code examples in the manual, the first—and possibly only—code examples a new programmer might see. In examples all over the manual are **Command1**, **Picture1**, **Text1**, and so on. Sometimes they do use these prefixes; sometimes they combine the prefix and the default name together into a weird hybrid.

The manual says there is nothing wrong with keeping the original default name. It does say it might be difficult to distinguish the **Command1** button on **MyForm** from the **Command1** button on **YourForm**. **Command1** on **MyForm**? **Command1** on **YourForm**? What are they trying to do, get us all killed? Just think, there are now real applications that have a form called **MyForm** with a command button called **Command1**. Does Microsoft actually thinks this is a good idea?

Actually, *all* the manuals think this is a good idea. Everywhere I turn there's that **Command1** again. One journal says it uses prefixes for controls in all but a few exceptions. Such exceptions include when the code is simple. Well, code is always simple, isn't it? Just one line after the other. Next thing you know you've written an entire application that some poor slob like me is going to have to maintain.

Now what was the key word in that last line? *Maintain.* Anybody can dash off some little VB application that will run. It's another thing altogether to write a large, integrated multiproject application that must be maintained, debugged, enhanced, and added to over time. I have had the misfortune of inheriting about 75 separate projects in a single Visual Basic application. I also have several other VB applications that include numerous individual projects. To top it all off, I'm not all that bright. How on earth do you handle all that? Well first of all you don't name anything **Command1**.

Let's adopt our first standard. It's really very simple. First, establish a prefixing scheme for the form and all control names. The prefix should be followed by a short descriptive name that describes the object's data, action or function.

Examples:

```
chk_active
```
Active status check box

```
cmd_exit
```
Command button that performs exit processing

```
frm_emp_rpt
```
Form that displays the employee report

```
lbl_status
```
Status label

```
mnu_file
```
File menu item

```
txt_EMP_NAME
```
text box for field **EMP_NAME**

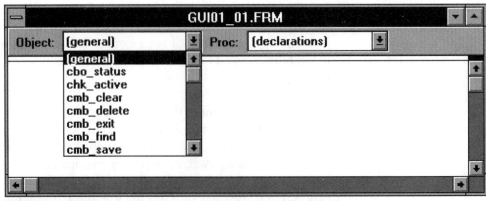

FIGURE 1.1 Prefixed controls lined up by type in the VB object box.

You can create whatever prefixing scheme you want, but the VB prefixes are good. All are three characters long. When you look at the list of controls in the object box they will line up nicely and in order by control type (Figure 1.1). Besides the standard VB controls, any additional VBX objects you use should also be given their own distinct prefix. I also use an underscore between the prefix and descriptive control name but this is personal preference.

Every control on the form should be set. I use an additional scheme for the name of any control that references a database field. This is covered in the "Cradle to Grave Variable Names" chapter. Now you know the type and purpose of an object referenced in a line of code without having to hunt down the actual object itself. **Command1?** Command *Yuck*.

FIRST MIDTERM EXAM:

Which of these is an acceptable name for a command button that saves data?

1. command1
2. save
3. cmb_save

Answer: 3.

You're catching on. You have now surpassed the standards for naming conventions of every VB book ever written. Congratulations.

Goulash and Other Variable Naming Techniques

Now we're getting somewhere. Let's take a quick look at variable names. There are three variable levels in VB:

☆ Local variables can be referenced only within the procedure in which they are declared.

☆ Module-level variables can be referenced by any procedure on the form or module in which they are declared.

☆ Global variables can be referenced anywhere in the project.

But you knew that already. Now read page 154 of the *Programmer's Guide for VB 3.0*. Here is an example of hell on earth. Look at all those variables: **A, B, M1, M2, X, Y, Z.** Do any of those variable names tell you anything about the type or scope? No. Is there any mention what a horror this is? No. Instead there's a happy little speech about shadows and which variable is running the show if they're all called **Temp**. Just think, there are now real applications that have global variables called **A** and **B**. Again I ask, does Microsoft actually think this is a good idea?

This situation is far more serious than blundering the control names. You cannot possibly hope to maintain a project of any size if you don't get dead serious about variable names. That this is glossed over in every single manual I read is something I find appalling. I once needed to do maintenance programming on an application that actually used **DW** as a global variable name. **DW**? **DW**! Spending time figuring out the scope of variable with a stupid name is a fun exercise in a textbook. Spending time figuring out the scope of variable with a stupid name in a production application is not. Misassigning a global variable because you thought is was local might cost you hours in agonizing debugging.

Let's adopt our second standard. It's really very simple: Establish a prefixing scheme for all the variables used in the application. The prefix should be state the variable's scope and its type.

One of the prefixing systems for variable names is called Hungarian Notation. Every variable is preceded by a two-digit code. The first digit is the scope of the variable. The second digit is the variable type.

Examples of the first letter in the prefix that describes the variable's scope:

    L: prefix to local variables
    F: prefix to form and module variables
    G: prefix to global variables
    A: prefix to variables passed into a routine as arguments

Examples of the second letter in the prefix that describes the variable's type:

    C: currency
    D: double
    I: integer
    L: long
    N: single (since S and I are used for other types)
    S: string
    V: variant

Let's put the two together and see what we get.

Examples:

```
av_name
```
Argument Variant *(item passed into a subroutine or function)*

```
fs_date
```
Form Level String

```
gs_name
```
Global String

```
li_id
```
Local Integer

Again, my personal preference is to use an underscore between the prefix and descriptive name. Here are a few variations on the notation scheme:

```
gs_name, fs_name, ls_name:
```
(scope) + (type) + (underscore) + (descriptive name)

```
gsName, fsName, lsName:
```
(scope) + (type) + (descriptive name, first letter uppercase)

```
gsname, fsname, lsname:
```
(scope) + (type) + (descriptive name)

Any of these three variations can be used instead with the VB data suffixes for data type instead of the second letter prefix.

```
g_name$, f_name$, l_name$:
```
(scope) + (underscore) + (descriptive name) + (VB type decl), etc.

Let's test an example:

```
Function ffn_math(ai_value As Integer) As Integer

      Dim li_value As Integer

      li_value = Int(100 * Rnd + 1)

      ffn_math = ((ai_value * li_value) + gi_value)/fi_value

End Function
```

Look at the last line of code. What does our naming convention tell us? The integer argument passed to the function is multiplied by a local integer variable. It's added to a global integer, then the whole mess is divided by a form level integer. Can you believe I got all that information out of that one line? But what about the shadows and five variables named **Temp** and all that other stuff? Our scheme has done away with it.

You can't reference a procedure's local variable from another procedure. Anytime you see a variable with the letter **L** in front of it, you know you're working with something you declared in the current procedure.

You can't reference a form/module variable from another form/module. Anytime you see a variable with the letter **F** in front of it, you know you're working with something you declared on the current form/module.

You can't reference a routine's argument variable from another routine. Anytime you see a variable with the letter **A** in front of it, you know you're working with something you passed in to the current routine.

Anytime you see a variable with the letter **G** in front of it, you know that the variable can be referenced from anywhere in the project.

You no longer have the situation where you can actually assign or reference a value to two variables that have exactly the same name. The variable **emp_id** does not exist on three levels. It exists as **gs_emp_id**, **fs_emp_id**, and **ls_emp_id**.

Object Variables

An object variable should use (scope) + (object type) {+ (name)} notation:

```
a_txt
```
text box control passed to a routine as an argument

```
l_grd
```
local grid

```
g_frm
```
global form

```
f_ctl
```
form-level generic control

Example:

```
Sub fsb_color_change(a_ctl_current As Control)

      a_ctl_current.BackColor = 0

End Sub
```

Question: I use the variant data type for everything. Do I still need that V everywhere?

Are you absolutely sure you'll never use another variable type? If not, then I'd stick with the V.

SECOND MIDTERM EXAM:

Which of these is an acceptable global string variable for **emp_id**?
1. **emp_id**
2. **g_emp_id**
3. **gs_emp_id**

Answer: 3.

Variables Passed to a Routine: No Argument

The most overlooked prefix is an argument passed into routines. I think it is a major oversight. Actually, I've never seen anybody but me prefix them so maybe I'm the one with the problem. By prefixing with the letter A + (type) + (name), you know immediately within the body of the subroutine or function that this is an argument passed in during the call.

Why is this such a big deal? The argument variable is the queen of the procedure. She is majestic and important. The routine exists to please her and act according to her value. Unprefixed, she looks like all the other local riffraff variables that live short, brutal little lives, then die at the end of the call. Don't cover her face. A + (type) + (name). Mine eyes dazzle.

Also remember that unless you declare an argument **ByVal**, it is passed by reference to the routine. This means that if you change that variable's value in the routine, it also changes its value in the calling procedure. If this is what you want to do, then fine; otherwise, you got real troubles.

Let's look at a code example with this side effect bug in it:

```
Function ffn_salary_projection(ac_salary As Currency) As Currency

        Dim li_value As Integer

        li_value = Int(100 * Rnd + 1)

        ac_salary = ac_salary * li_value

        ffn_salary_projection= ac_salary

End Function
```

A call to this function might look like this:

```
Dim lc_salary As Currency

Dim lc_salary_future      As Currency


lc_salary = 30000

lc_salary_future = ffn_salary_projection(lc_salary)


'{Now lc_salary value is sent over to payroll}

MsgBox(Str(lc_salary))   'lc_salary changed unintentionally
```

Now, did you really want the value of **lc_salary** to change? If not, the prefixing scheme quickly shows the problem. The argument passed to the routine is being assigned a value that it's carrying back to the calling procedure. Anytime I write or see **ac_salary = *anything***, I know the code is changing the argument variable and maybe I better think again. I should use a local variable if I need the results of **ac_salary * li_value**. (Yeah, yeah, you can do the whole function in one statement with no variables. Hey, I'm trying to make a point here.)

If I had passed this variable in as **x** or **numval**, I probably wouldn't have spotted the error. If this routine were hundreds of lines long, I guarantee I wouldn't remember that **x** was an argument variable. This might cause a mistaken assignment. This might cause a bug in another routine that will take forever to find.

The other benefit of the convention becomes obvious when you find that **ac_salary** has a ridiculous value; you're reminded that the problem might be with the procedure that called this routine. Maybe the error isn't with this routine at all; instead the calling procedure is passing in an incorrect value. This has been my experience numerous times. No way I'd have figured it out without the proper notation.

Now if you're really conscientious, you can differentiate between variables passed by value and variables passed by reference. You can use **acr_salary** for reference and **acv_salary** for value. Then you're absolutely sure that the line of code you're looking at is making an assignment to a value that will be carried back to the calling procedure. I won't press this issue since nobody ever prefixes argument values at all, and variables are usually defaulted to pass by reference. I'd be happy if you just put **A + (type)**, but the extra option is certainly there for the taking. Also consider spending the extra time to declare argument variables **ByVal** if their calling values should not be changed, thus preventing these side effect assignments. If the previous routine was declared like this:

```
Function ffn_salary_projection (ByVal ac_salary As Currency) As Currency
```

then **lc_salary** would not have changed in the calling procedure.

Of course no manual or book would ever dream of using any convention for argument variables. Go through every VB book you own. See what they use. Most likely they use x, y, and z. Whose maintaining that code? Argument prefixing has saved me in debugging so many times that if I was allowed to keep just one piece of the variable naming convention scheme, this would be it.

FINAL EXAM:

Which of these is an acceptable string variable argument to a subroutine?

1. **emp_id**
2. **s_emp_id**

3. **as_emp_id**

Answer: 3.

Routine Names: Don't Call Me Baby

We're on a roll. Our naming scheme includes controls and variables. What's next? Subroutine and function names, of course. Gee, I've never seen those prefixed before. Usually a book gives a code example like this:

```
z=Sum(x,y)

Sort_Recs
```

Now what is **Sum**? Is it an internal VB function? Did you write it? Where might it be? How about **Sort_Recs**? What is it doing there sitting like a lump? Probably a subroutine call. Awful.

Let's adopt our third standard. It's really very simple, too: Establish a prefixing scheme for all the subroutines and functions used in the application.

The prefix should state the routine's scope and type.

Form-level subroutines and functions are private to the form. These routines can be called only from that form. Module-level routines are either private to the module or global. If a module-level routine is prefaced with the reserved word **Private**, it can be called only from that module. Otherwise, the routine can be called from anywhere in the project. Therefore, we need to distinguish the two types of routines: local routines private to the form or module, and global routines.

Here's one possible prefix scheme for routine scope:
- **F:** form and module level routines (thus carrying over the convention of using F for form/module level variables)
- **G:** global routine

Here's one possible prefix scheme for routine type:
- **FN:** function
- **SB:** subroutine

Examples of routines named using this scheme:

```
Form/Module-Level Routines: (scope) + (routine type) + routine name
```

```
        function ffn_save_recs

        sub fsb_save_data


Global Routines: (scope) + (routine type) + routine name

        function gfn_save_recs

        sub gsb_save_data
```

Functions can include an additional prefix which is the variable type that it returns.

Example:

```
(scope) + (routine type) + (return value type) + routine name

        Function ffn_i_ParseItems - Returns integer value

        Function gfn_s_ParseItems - Returns string value
```

Since nobody ever prefixes subroutines or functions at all, I won't insist on including the return variable prefix, but, again, it's there for the taking. As always, I use the underscore for clarity but this is personal preference.

Please understand the key point in this naming convention. Subroutines and functions are not the same thing. Functions return a value, subroutines do not. They are called differently and thus should be named differently.

File Names: I'm Different and Proud

Let's finish with a naming scheme for all the actual files in a project. VB does a good job assigning the three-digit extension to all files in the project: MAK for the project file, FRM for forms, BAS for code modules. You're responsible for the rest. You don't want to have your application's projects use the default names FORM1.FRM, MODULE1.BAS, PROJECT1.BAS, and so on. Every file in an application should have a unique name.

Use a naming convention for all the files associated with a single project. One possible scheme is a six- or seven-letter root name followed by a number. This allows for multiple forms and modules in a project. The specifics of the root name will depend on the size and type of the application. Use the root name for the MAK, BAS, and FRM files, and store all the files for the project in a subdirectory also similarly named.

Example:
EMPRPT—Employee Report Project
All files reside in c:\app_xxx**EMPRPT**\
        EMPRPT.MAK—Project File
        EMPRPT01.FRM—Form
        EMPRPT02.FRM—Form
        EMPRPT01.BAS—Code Module

In the event that a file is lost or accidentally saved to the wrong location, the naming scheme will help you guide it back to its proper home. If you stick with the FORM1.FRM, MODULE1.BAS, PROJECT1.BAS naming system, a file accidentally copied to the wrong area could overwrite an existing file in another project. Someone will be really mad when they get back from lunch.

Cradle to Grave Variable Names

I use the following technique. I don't know if anyone else uses it, but I would never do it any other way. Trust me, it will save you from going insane in big programs. When you begin the typical project you have a data dictionary that shows the tables your program will access and the fields in each table.

Example:

EMPLOYEE table

EMP_ID	Integer
F_NAME	Char(10)
L_NAME	Char(30)
M_INIT	Char(1)
STATUS_CD	Integer
COMMENTS	Char(100)

I suggest you use the actual database field name as the basis for the names of all objects, variables, arrays, function, constants, and so on that are associated with it. I call this cradle to grave variable naming. By looking at the data dictionary, you know the root of any name associated with the field.

The Wrong Way

I've seen and needed to maintain a program like this:
Name in data dictionary is DATA_VL
Text box control is named txt_DATA_VALUE
Hold variable to store its original value is called fs_DATA_VAL
Array of this item used for other purposes called
         fs_array_DATAVALUE()

Arghhh! The program had over two dozen such variables, each with a slight twist in each incarnation. With this method, every time you want to make a change you say, "Now what was the name of the text box?" Then you have to go looking for it. Then you have the same problem with the control name for another variable, and you have to go recheck it. Soon you're spending all your time hunting around to get whichever twisted variation of the name was used.

I spend time up front getting the names consistent with the data dictionary, and I am forever grateful each time I need to make additional changes. The following code is meaningless, but it shows the naming technique.

```
Dim fs_DATA_VL As String

Dim fs_array_DATA_VL(10) As String

Const C_DATA_VL = 1

Sub fsb_example()

    If txt_DATA_VL.Text <> fs_DATA_VL Then

        grd_data.Col = C_DATA_VL

        fs_array_DATA_VL(1) = grd_data.Text

    End If

End Sub
```

I prefer to capitalize the field name when using this naming scheme. Variables that don't reference data fields (and thus don't use cradle-to-grave notation) are set in all lowercase. This way, when I see the variable **fs_DATA_VL** when scanning my code, I know immediately that it is concerned with an actual data field. Once again, this is a personal preference, but I find making this distinction very helpful.

Using a standard control naming scheme in combination with cradle-to-grave data field names places your application on very sturdy ground. Any programmer armed with the control naming standards and the data dictionary can go into another person's project and instantly know the name of any data control. Just think of the awful naming discord that might have been. We've come a very long way indeed.

This combination also makes starting up the project much faster. I begin every new assignment with the data dictionary right next to the monitor. Just a quick glance at the sheet during coding reminds me that the name of the text box for the employee's first name is **txt_F_NAME**. With this technique in place I spend my time concentrating on programming, not on guessing games.

Constantinople

VB 3.0 comes with a file called CONSTANT.TXT that is a set of symbolic constants. Amazingly enough, most VB book authors have discovered this file and use these constants in their examples instead of hardcoding the numbers. Considering how miserable most of these books are with the rest of their naming conventions, this is quite a pleasant surprise. The contents of CONSTANT.TXT should be part of your own applications, either as a separate file or included in a global BAS file. These constants should be used instead of hardcodes whenever possible (hardcodes are the actual numbers themselves but sound meaner). Take 10 minutes and scroll through this file to see what constants you can start using. I always find one I missed each time I run though it.

Using these VB constants will greatly aid in the readability of your code. But don't hesitate to declare your own whenever appropriate. One of the best uses of a constant is as a substitute for a column number when referring to data fields in a grid, spreadsheet, or dynaset. This is unbelievably useful in prototype programs that often require fields be added, removed, or reordered. The technique was explained to me by a programmer who was being driven insane during application review. During each review cycle a different column order was requested in a spreadsheet object. I've been in many similar situations myself. Use the following technique and take the evil out of these encounters.

Example:
SQL statement retrieves data from the EMPLOYEE in some kind of display data grid object.

```
SELECT
        EMP_ID, F_NAME, M_INIT, L_NAME, STATUS_CD, COMMENTS
FROM
        EMPLOYEE
```

Each field is retrieved into a column in this data grid.

Now let's say this data must be copied to VB controls for editing. You can make typical assignments like these:

```
txt_EMP_ID.Text = grd_data(li_row, 1).Text

txt_F_NAME.Text = grd_data(li_row, 2).Text

txt_M_INIT.Text = grd_data(li_row, 3).Text

txt_L_NAME.Text = grd_data(li_row, 4).Text

txt_STATUS_CD.Text = grd_data(li_row, 5).Text

txt_COMMENTS.Text = grd_data(li_row, 6).Text
```

(This assignment method is fictitious—it's used for clarity.)

The problem with this method becomes apparent when users decide to change the order of the columns in the display grid. Let's say the new SQL retrieve order changes to **L_NAME**, **F_NAME**, **M_INIT**, **EMP_ID**, **COMMENTS**, **STATUS_CD**. Since your program is based on the assumption that a specific column in the data grid corresponds to a specific field, you have to go through all your code and reassign the numbers. Here's the new code:

```
txt_EMP_ID.Text = grd_data(li_row, 4).Text

txt_F_NAME.Text = grd_data(li_row, 2).Text

txt_M_INIT.Text = grd_data(li_row, 3).Text

txt_L_NAME.Text = grd_data(li_row, 1).Text

txt_STATUS_CD.Text = grd_data(li_row, 6).Text

txt_COMMENTS.Text = grd_data(li_row, 5).Text
```

This number reassignment stuff can get very tedious and error prone in a large program, especially when a major column reordering is made. It's just slightly inconvenient in this simple example. I've had programs that had a whole lot of code depending upon certain fields being in certain columns. During the review cycle of one of these programs a new field needed to be added and displayed as the first column of the data grid. The agony of hardcoding the column numbers hit home. This brutal request effectively destroyed the whole fragile scheme.

I converted the whole thing to refer to constants (which is much harder than if you start out using them) and now it's one beautiful vision. Reorder all you want, you idiots. It'll take me less than a minute to change. I've won! ha. ha. ha.

Here's the solution to the reassignment chaos. Declare these constants:

```
'Data Grid Columns

Const C_L_NAME = 1

Const C_F_NAME = 2

Const C_M_INIT = 3

Const C_EMP_ID = 4

Const C_COMMENTS = 5

Const C_STATUS_CD = 6
```

Now look at the code:

```
txt_EMP_ID.Text = grd_data(li_row, C_EMP_ID).Text
```

```
txt_F_NAME.Text = grd_data(li_row, C_F_NAME).Text

txt_M_INIT.Text = grd_data(li_row, C_M_INIT).Text

txt_L_NAME.Text = grd_data(li_row, C_L_NAME).Text

txt_STATUS_CD.Text = grd_data(li_row, C_STATUS_CD).Text

txt_COMMENTS.Text = grd_data(li_row, C_COMMENTS).Text
```

Make all code refer to the constant instead of hardcoding the number. Then any future reordering changes can be made just to the constant declarations, not through all the code. The added benefit is that the code becomes self-documenting. I won't remember what field is in column 17 of a grid a month from now. A maintenance programmer will have no idea to begin with. Refer to it as **C_TELE_NUM** and we're getting somewhere. I again suggest you use the name in the data dictionary as the root name of the constant. With a large number of columns, this scheme will make it much easier to make assignments.

Despite the belief of some mathematicians, God did not invent the integers. The more sensible deity opted instead to assign them to global constants which are now used throughout the universe. Yeah, like God uses hardcodes. Get real.

Option Explicit: Order from Chaos

After establishing a strict variable naming standard, there is one vital action that must be carried out. Set **Option Explicit** on all your forms and module files. This requires you to declare all your variables explicitly. Don't even consider not doing it. Set this permanently in your VB Environment with the menu item **Options - Environment : Require Variable Declaration = Yes** (Figure 1.2). Do this immediately.

Every book and manual seems to consider **Option Explicit** rather lightly. You may want to use it. Maybe you could try it. Just try a little bite to make grandma happy. Let me add my own gentle aside. You may want to embroider it on a pillow.

If you do not use **Option Explicit**, your project is doomed.

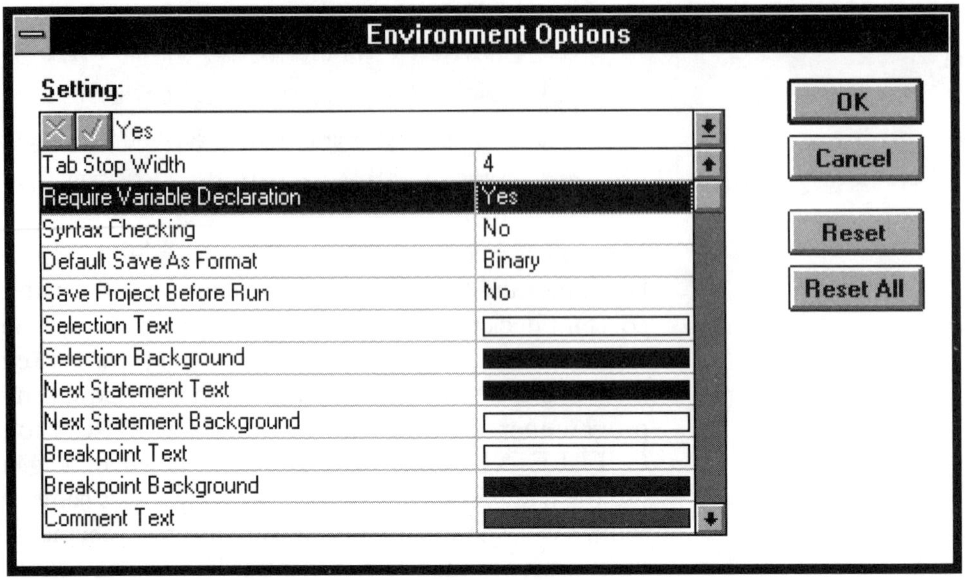

FIGURE 1.2 Option explicit set as a default environment option.

I had an interview with a company during which the project leader said he didn't require the programmers to use Option Explicit because they were used to QuickBasic and didn't like the idea. I don't like the idea of a program returning garbage if I misspell a variable name. Look at the following example and get scared straight.

Example (Without Option Explicit):

```
PayCheck = 1000
Inc = PayChek * (.25)
PayCheck = PayCheck + Inc
MsgBox (PayCheck)
```

Result:

```
1000
```

So much for that big raise. I make spelling mistakes like this all the time. You can imagine how disastrous the results could be. Please begin this standard immediately and it will be painless. Declaring variables will become natural (if it isn't already), and the extra time spent will pay off. If you have to convert a FRM or BAS file to **Option Explicit** later, it will drive you crazy. Start out crazy and reap the rewards.

Naming Conventions Summary

When you go on an interview for a programming position, ask about the company's naming conventions. Most places I talk to have none. "We let the programmers do what they want." Some bravely state, "We try to use the letter G before the global variables." Their entire standard naming scheme can be summed up in a single letter—G. Well gee, that's pretty meager guys.

Without a comprehensive naming scheme, everything looks the same. Each line of code is a new puzzle to solve. Is **Sum** a form-level subroutine? A global function? Maybe it's a local variable or a text box. Possibly it's all of the above. If there's no naming conventions, it's likely that **Sum** refers to different things in different situations. That's torture code. Once you get into the maintenance phase of a project, those lines of code are going to tear through your skin like little strips of barbed wire.

None of the conventions I explained should seem like a punishment. They are meant to help you—now and especially six months from now. You're going to need a solid base of naming conventions if a large project has any hopes of surviving. Don't rush through this step of development to get started playing with the 3-D Juice Bar VBX. Agonize over it. Scream at one another. Draw blood. Don't accept my conventions. Make your own decision about the naming scheme for each and every item I've mentioned.

Now, pick *one* standard naming scheme and stick with it. Having two naming standards, like they do in the VB manual, means you have no standard. When you've decided on a standard, embrace it. Passionately. These standards should be written up and distributed to all programmers. They are to be followed with no exceptions.

What do you get for all your trouble? Just one thing. An application that can be maintained. By establishing naming conventions, most of the horror scenario described in the opening to this section has gone away. You can actually survive when you inherit someone's project.

There is no greater horror than to end up with an project that's written like one of the samples included with VB. After you've absorbed what I've said about naming conventions, pop into one of those babies and look around. These guys can't properly name a routine or variable to save their lives. I would quit my job if I had to maintain code like that. I myself use to write such drivel. I look at the first application I did and feel quite ashamed. Thank God it's no longer in production. There's no way I could ever maintain it. Honestly, this naming stuff is what's going to keep you sane when all hell breaks loose.

(Embrace the standards passionately? Good grief. I've really got to get out more.)

2

THE GLOBAL ARENA

The following sections focus on some global aspects of an application, including global routines, BAS files, forms, variables, standard processing methods, and VBXs. Don't focus on the particular techniques themselves, but on the concepts behind them. By working through these ideas yourself before beginning an application, you help ensure consistency in program operation and ease later programming tasks and maintenance.

Global Routines: The Lazy Man's Friend

I don't know why most VB book authors love to show all the code examples at the field level. "Look at all this lovely code you can cut and paste all over the place. If you're really a wild man maybe you can try writing some of it at the form level." Hey buddy, I don't want to copy, I don't want to paste, I really don't want to write the code in the first place. Are you getting paid by the word or something? I want a single black box call. I'm busy, dammit, don't waste my time by making me write edit checks at the field level. That's right my friends, let's get angry, and let's write some global routines.

Global routines help ensure consistency in your coding, reduce the amount of code in the project, and relieve much of the drudgery involved in rote programming. Once you have a healthy set of global routines, you can focus on the hard stuff, not reinvent the coding wheel. To determine what would make a good global routine, you don't need any brains, you just need to be lazy. Let's look at a process that everybody has been writing since the dawn of time (or the dawn of VB at least). The old chestnut of finding and highlighting a value in a list box.

Here the program must find and highlight the current user in the list box. The processing would be the same for the combo box.

```
Dim li_ctr As Integer

lst_EMP_NAME.ListIndex = -1 'Deselect current item

        'If current value doesn't match then nothing will be
            ⇨highlighted

For li_ctr = 0 To (lst_EMP_NAME.ListCount - 1)

        If lst_EMP_NAME.List(li_ctr) = fs_EMP_NAME Then

            'Found It

            lst_EMP_NAME.ListIndex = li_ctr

            Exit For          'Don't Look Anymore

        End If

Next li_ctr


If lst_EMP_NAME.ListIndex = -1 Then

        MsgBox("Employee name not found.")

End If
```

Ahh, the list box. Who invented these awful things? They look nice, but underneath are little monsters waiting to snatch the unwary. The whole find process is weird: start with 0, end with ListCount-1, check List, assign ListIndex. Yuck. Every time I write this little loop I do something wrong. Then I have to muck through the manual. That's when the global routine light bulb comes on. Why am I writing yet another version of a standard process when I could be running naked through the halls?

Here's a first stab at globalization:

```
Function gfn_lst_finditem (a_lst As ListBox, as_value As
    ⇨String) As Integer

    Dim li_ctr As Integer


    a_lst.ListIndex = -1
'deselect current item - if current value doesn't match then
    ⇨nothing will be highlighted
    gfn_lst_finditem = -1 'no match found yet
    For li_ctr = 0 To (a_lst.ListCount - 1)
        If a_lst.List(li_ctr) = as_value Then
            a_lst.ListIndex = li_ctr
```

```
                    gfn_lst_finditem = li_ctr 'found a match

                    Exit For

            End If

    Next li_ctr

End Function
```

```
Calling procedure:

    If gfn_lst_finditem (lst_EMP_NAME, fs_EMP_NAME) = -1 Then

        MsgBox("Employee name not found.")

    End If
```

That little routine is going to save me a lot of time and effort. Look at what the calling procedure is now. It's small and readable. The best thing about it is I never have to figure out that code again. I can forget about how the list box works. I really don't care. Spending time converting a common process into a global generic routine, whether it takes an hour, a day, or a week is always worth the effort. My boss recently wrote a generic global report routine. You pass it some setup information and a data grid and its off generating a report. I have no idea how it works and I don't want to know. The routine was agony to write (and I mean agony) but now that it's done no one has to go through that horrible process again. This is really what you're doing when writing one of these routines: forcing all the pain and torture of programming into one spot. I scroll through some of the more complicated global routines and can still hear the screams.

We get a whole lot for our trouble:

- ☆ **Reduce common errors and standardize processing.** Much of standard processing is simple but somewhat tricky. This list box selection routine is a good example. There are a lot of little things that can go wrong here. Six programmers will write the code six different ways. Some of this code will work perfectly, some won't. Why risk the effects of these simple errors? A global routine will perform the same all the time. This consistency in processing is vital to convincing users that your system is a nice place to work. Little inconsistencies add up and destroy users' confidence in the application.

- ☆ **Centralized bug fixes or enhancements.** If there happens to be a problem with the way this routine works, or some genius figures out a way to make it run better, it's changed in one place. This sure beats tracking down a fatal coding flaw in dozens of applications. Write once, fix once.

☆ **Improve efficiency, clarity, and speed of coding.** With a good set of global routines, the grunt work is done for you. You spend your time on the core logic. Later on, your code is far more readable. When you look at a block of code in one of your procedures, the important logic stands out. Code doesn't break when you drop it, so don't wrap your fine china in layers of crumpled newspaper.

What's an easier mix of code to wade through?
> 10 lines of simple stuff
> 10 important lines
> 10 lines of simple stuff

or
> 1 line calling a routine containing the simple stuff
> 10 important lines
> 1 line calling a routine containing the other simple stuff

That's a nice meaty sandwich. All that tasty roast beef isn't hidden between two big stale rolls.

Later on, we will look at setting up the global BAS files that will contain these routines. First, though, let's look at the programming logic structures and techniques I have found most useful in writing these global routines.

First of All, Standards

Global routines are the place to really pull out all the stops for adhering to standards:

☆ Option Explicit, always a must.

☆ Proper prefixing for the routine name and variables (please, please, please prefix variables passed into the routine).

Example:

```
Function gfn_check_for_chr (as_data As String, as_chr As
  ⇨String) As Integer
```

☆ Well-commented. This is especially important since programmers need to understand how and why they should use a routine they didn't write themselves. This is covered more thoroughly in Chapter 5, in the section titled "**No Comment.**"

★ Constants where appropriate to increase readability and ease maintenance. Use the constants from CONSTANT.TXT, and consider using your own constants for any positional numeric information like data columns. If a function returns different numeric status codes, consider using constants within the routine to help clarify what's going on. This very useful for maintenance. Following are two statements within a function called **gfn_error_status**. Both statements return an error code. Ask yourself which is easier to read and maintain.

```
gfn_error_status = -23
```

or

```
gfn_error_status = BAD_FILE_NAME
```

★ Error-trapping if applicable and deemed necessary. Functions can return an error code if the processing failed so the calling procedure can decide whether to abort any further actions. Subroutines can display a message box warning of the a problem. Some specific error traps are shown later in this chapter.

A Control or Form Passed into a Routine As an Argument

This is the most useful and powerful technique in writing global routines. We saw this in our first global example.

```
Function gfn_lst_finditem (a_lst As ListBox, as_value As String)
   ⇨As Integer
```

The argument variable **a_lst** is a pointer to the control passed into the function. Any of the operations we might perform on a specific list box using in-line code can now be done in this procedure. Wow, this is powerful stuff. We can change an object's properties, get its current value, or set a new value. Any standard control coding can be bumped up to a global process. Why keep writing all these little code routines if we don't have to?

Controls can be passed as an argument by their specific control type or by the generic type *control*. The **a_lst** argument is specific and will accept only a list box as an argument. Try anything else and the program won't compile. The generic *control* argument will let anybody in. This gives enormous flexibility. Since list boxes and combo boxes find items in the same way, we can convert the previous function so we can pass it either one. Just change the argument:

```
Function gfn_lst_finditem (a_lst As Control, as_value As String)
    ⇨As Integer
```

Now we can pass in a list or combo box. Of course now we can also pass in a grid or check box and get a "Property Not Found" error. I think the benefit of having just one routine to handle both cases is worth the risk. If your global routines are well named and commented, you're unlikely to get such errors. Just in case, we'll cover an error trap technique later on.

Here's an example of a generic form argument value:

```
Sub gsb_form_center(a_frm As Form)
    a_frm.Left = (screen.Width - a_frm.Width) / 2 ' Centers form
        ⇨horizontally
    a_frm.Top = (screen.Height - a_frm.Height) / 2 ' Centers form
        ⇨vertically
End Sub
```

Call from the **Form_Load** event:

```
Call gsb_form_center(Me) 'centers the form on the screen
```

It's pretty simple code, but why write it twice?

ActiveControl

I have seen global routines that do not pass in the control as an argument. Instead they refer to the control using the **ActiveControl** command. Here a small part of the code used to allow only numeric entries into a text box.

```
If Instr(Screen.ActiveControl.Text,".") > 0 Then
    'Already Have One Decimal Point - Disallow
    KeyAscii = 0
End If
```

I like the **ActiveControl** command, but why build in a limitation? Designing a routine that only works on the current active control limits its functionality. Don't make any assumptions in a global routine. Provided that the routine declares the control as the generic type (as control), the **ActiveControl** command can instead be passed into the routine as an argument.

```
Sub gsb_control_magic(a_ctl As Control)
    'Does something wonderful
```

```
End Sub

Call gsb_control_magic(Screen.ActiveControl)
```

Controls Collection and Forms Collection

I have honestly never used either of the these in a routine. They do look promising though. If you are trying to perform a similar process on every loaded form or every control on a form, these are the guys to see. I guess they are VB internal arrays. Don't worry about it. Just know that you can use them to loop through and play with every control on a form or all loaded forms. Of course, this processing starts at 0 and ends with (Count-1). I really hate that. I combined the two collections into one silly example.

```
Sub gsb_black_out()

    'Set BackColor Of Everything To Black

    Dim li_curr_frm As Integer

    Dim li_curr_ctl As Integer


    'Sweep Through All Forms

    For li_curr_frm = 0 To (Forms.Count - 1)

        Forms(li_curr_frm).BackColor = BLACK 'change each form's
            ⇨backcolor


        'Sweep Through Each Control On Form

        For li_curr_ctl = 0 To (Forms(li_curr_frm).Controls.Count - 1)

            Forms(li_curr_frm).Controls(li_curr_ctl).BackColor
                ⇨= BLACK     'change color

        Next li_curr_ctl

    Next li_curr_frm

End Sub
```

If TypeOf *object* Is *objecttype* Then

The syntax of this command is strange. I can never figure it out, and then I have to unearth the manual. Strangeness aside, it is very useful. Consider it the good friend of the generic *control* argument. With this command we can now determine the type of the control and act accordingly. The following routine will clear out the value in a control. The process isn't the same for each type so we get some help from our weird friend.

```
Sub gsb_clear_ctl(a_ctl As Control)

    If TypeOf a_ctl Is TextBox Then
        a_ctl.Text = ""

    ElseIf TypeOf a_ctl Is Label Then
        a_ctl.Caption = ""

    ElseIf TypeOf a_ctl Is ComboBox Then
        a_ctl.ListIndex = -1

    End If

End Sub
```

The structure of TypeOf logic is limited to what you see in the preceding routine. You can't use it as the expression in my beloved Select Case statement or try anything fancy like this:

```
If TypeOf a_ctl Is ComboBox or ListBox Then
    a_ctl.ListIndex = -1
End If
```

Now you can add an error trap to routines that only process certain control types even though the control argument is generic. Here's an error trap for our first function that works only with combo and list boxes.

```
Function gfn_lst_finditem (a_lst As Control, as_value As String)
    ⇨As Integer

    If TypeOf a_lst Is ComboBox Then
        'O.K. - fall through to function

    ElseIf TypeOf a_lst Is ListBox Then
        'O.K. - fall through to function
    Else
        MsgBox("Wrong control type passed to gfn_lst_finditem.")
        gfn_lst_finditem = -1
        Exit Function
    End If
    'Rest Off The Routine
```

Select Case

The Select Case statement is used when a routine must perform different code under different situations. I prefer it to If-Then-Else logic statements even for only two options. If you start off using a Select Case statement your routine has room to grow. You can add ElseIfs to the If-Then-Else logic, but to me it's just ugly. Provided you're evaluating a single expression you can rewrite the logic to Select Case. Here's a simple routine to show the technique:

```
Function gfn_integer_math(ai_one As Integer, ai_two As Integer,
    as_operation As String) As Integer

    Select Case as_operation

        Case "+"    'Add
              gfn_integer_math = ai_one + ai_two


        Case "-"    'Subtract
              gfn_integer_math = ai_one - ai_two

    End Select


End Function
```

Maybe I'm weird, but doesn't that look elegant? It's easy to follow. The evaluated condition is displayed once at the top of the loop. Each option gets its own little perch. We can graduate to the third grade and add more options yet still maintain our urbane composure:

```
    Select Case as_operation

        Case "+"    'Add
                gfn_integer_math = ai_one + ai_two
        Case "-"    'Subtract
                gfn_integer_math = ai_one - ai_two

        Case "/"    'Divide
                gfn_integer_math = ai_one / ai_two

        Case "*"    'Multiple
                gfn_integer_math = ai_one * ai_two
    End Select
```

Here's a routine that you might use if your application saves check box results as Y or N values in the database. After determining the current field value, this function could be called to assign the check box.

```
Sub gsb_set_chk(a_chk As CheckBox, as_value As String)

    Select Case UCase(as_value)

        Case "Y"

            a_chk.value = CHECKED

        Case "N"

            a_chk.value=UNCHECKED

        Case Else

            MsgBox("Improper check box data value.")

    End Select
End Sub
```

Calling procedure:

```
Call gsb_set_chk(chk_ACTIVE, fs_ACTIVE)
```

I had code to do this in all my programs until I wised up and made it a global process. My in-line code would have looked like this:

```
If fs_ACTIVE = "Y" Then
    chk_ACTIVE.value = CHECKED
Else
    chk_ACTIVE.value = UNCHECKED
End If
```

The global routine is a definite enhancement. My lazy in-line code will still run with weird data. I probably didn't type all the nice code that's in the global routine each time. I gotta get a move on. If my logic mistakenly assigns **fs_ACTIVE** incorrectly, perhaps to another field's value, I won't notice the problem. My logic just says, "Nope, **fs_ACTIVE** isn't Y, uncheck that box and keep on going." This bug will hang around unnoticed until the most inconvenient time. I once spend two hours tracking down a bug like this. This is why I prefer the Select Case over a single If-Then statement. I specify each case explicitly then add an additional Case Else for error trapping. If that error message box comes up, I know something's wrong with the code.

Bait and Switch

Don't write two or more routines that are mirrors of each other except that one condition is different. I have seen this done on both the form and global levels. There is no need to write separate routines to make things enabled and disabled, visible and invisible, and so on. Instead, use a switch variable for different states. Here's another silly routine to demonstrate the technique:

```
Sub gsb_ctl_enabled(a_ctl As Control, ai_Enabled As Integer)

    a_ctl.Enabled = ai_Enabled

End Sub
```

Calling procedure:

```
Call gsb_ctl_enabled(txt_EMP_NAME, true)

Call gsb_ctl_enabled(txt_EMP_NAME, false)
```

Once again, our goal is a single-point approach. Take nothing for granted in a global routine. Don't hardcode anything. Pass in everything that might be a variable. I've seen people write two global routines that were identical except for the database name. No assumptions I tell ya. If the condition can vary, then pass it in.

I don't want any more code than is absolutely necessary. It happens every time with these multiprong routines. A problem is found and corrected in only one of them, while the other rogues get away and wait to harass another victim.

Noun-Verb Name Format

Before you run off and start writing these routines, decide on a standard format for the names. I prefer a noun-verb form:

```
Sub gsb_grd_clear
Sub gsb_grd_copy
Sub gsb_grd_delete
Sub gsb_lst_clear
Sub gsb_lst_copy
Sub gsb_lst_delete
```

You get the idea. When you scroll though the BAS file that contains the routines, they fall into a sensibly ordered list. If you prefer to use verb-noun, go ahead. Just don't mix them. It's frustrating trying to remember that to clear a grid you call **gsb_grd_clear**, but to copy it you use **gsb_copy_grd**. Once again, I'm lazy and don't want to be bothered remembering these sundry things when I'm in the middle of coding.

To Subroutine or Not to Subroutine

Carefully consider whether to use a subroutine or a function for each routine. Functions give the added advantage of being able to return a value. The success/failure of the operation can be returned. The calling program may not want to continue if the global routine failed to perform its desired task.

Last of All

Think as generically as possible. We want to get as much use out of these routines as possible. The way to get good at writing generic routines is to go through a VB book or manual and look at the code examples. Of course, everything will be processing at the lowest level possible. Look at the code, ask "Why should I keep writing this over and over?" and try to rewrite it as routine that will work on a grand scale. Start with my suggestions then improve on them. As always, I'm just pointing the way. Go ahead and leave me in the dust. There will be no moments more precious than the ones you save by calling your slick routines.

The Mighty BAS

Now that we have a handle on writing generic routines, let's figure out where to put them all. You want to develop a set of BAS files containing global routines that can be used in any application in your current programming environment as early in the development process as possible. Have everyone in the development group give ideas of likely candidates for global processes.

I think the best bet is to create a number of small BAS files developed for specific operations. In my current development environment we have a number of gobal BAS files devoted to separate processes. However, we have one BAS file, which has been added to over time, that is just called UTILITY. This BAS is really too large and generic for my taste. It has so many routines that cover so many different processes that you really can't remember them all or care to scroll the list to see if they exist. As a result, you write your own version at the form level and frustrate the whole process.

This is a benefit that a C programmer has over a Visual Basic programmer (besides a higher status in the community). There is a large library of include files already written for many C processes. But don't worry, a small set of global BAS files with good generic functions is not that hard to write.

The following is a short list of possible files. Of course, you know best what you need. Even if you don't have the time to write any routines in your generic BAS files, creating the empty husks in a global area is a very good base for future development. Their hollow halls will echo with your foresight and ambition (oh, brother).

MSGBOX.BAS

Wadda I need that for? One primary way your application communicates its needs, demands, and achievements is through the **MsgBox** call. The presentation of your app will be enhanced if you keep the messages consistent throughout.

Try to avoid this situation: When a user tries to exit a form without saving changes to data, the following message box appears:

App 1. Do you want to save the changes? (With Yes/No/Cancel Buttons)

App 2. Save Changes? (With Yes/No Buttons)

App 3. You have made changes and didn't save. OK? (With Yes/No Buttons)

App 4. Exit without saving the data? (With Yes/No/Cancel Buttons)

Get the idea? Subtle anarchy. The situation isn't critical, but I bet if these guys built a coffee table, each leg would be a different size. The application gets a chance to open its mouth and it says, "Nobody's in charge and I'm loving it!"

The **MsgBox** function is actually a tricky little thing. When I wrote **MsgBoxes** using in-line code, I always switched the places for the title and message. Adding an icon and setting the buttons involves some math. Don't waste your time. Write it once and forget about it. We'll look at two examples. You can base the rest of what you need on them.

A subroutine call is fine for most messages.

```
Sub gsb_MSGBOX_Information(as_msg As String)

    MsgBox as_msg, MB_ICONINFORMATION, "Information"

End Sub
```

Calling procedure:

```
Call gsb_MSGBOX_Information("File processing complete.")
```

We write a function call when the message box returns a conditional value.

```
Function gfn_MSGBOX_YesNoCancel(as_msg As String) As Integer

    gfn_MSGBOX_YesNoCancel = MsgBox(as_msg, MB_ICONQUESTION
        ⇨+ MB_YESNOCANCEL, "Question")

End Function
```

Calling procedure:

```
If gfn_MSGBOX_YesNoCancel("Continue?") = IDYES Then

    Call fsb_process_file

End If
```

VBX_Name.BAS

I suggest you create separate BAS files for any complicated VBXs you might have. These include grids, graphs, spreadsheets, and database add-ons. I currently have a couple of these files, and I use routines from them every day. I beat this subject to death later in the section "Care And Feeding of a VBX."

GLOBALS.BAS

This BAS file contains no routines. It includes only global variables and constants used throughout your applications.

This is the place to put the contents of the VB3 file CON-STANT.TXT. Put all the global variables here that will replace any hardcoded paths for data, database name, server, and so on. See "The Global Variable: Pathway to Exotic Data Locales" later in this chapter for the reasons why.

SQL.BAS

For any special routines you need to perform your SQL calls—routines to perform SELECT, INSERT, UPDATE, DELETE, and other SQL commands.

Include any procedures needed to login to the SQL database.

The size and utility of this BAS depends on the database add-on you're using to process SQL calls.

FILE_IO.BAS

For routines used to process flat files and generic DOS command processing.
gfn_FileExists
gfn_DirExists
gfn_get_data_dir
gfn_get_INI_value

Example:

```
Function gfn_FileExists (as_filename As String) As Integer

    Dim li_file_num As Integer

    li_file_num = FreeFile
    On Error Resume Next

    Open as_filename For Input Access Read Shared As li_file_num
    If Err = 0 Then
        gfn_FileExists = True     'No Error - File Exists
        Close li_file_num
    Else
        gfn_FileExists = False  'Error - File Doesn't Exist
    End If
End Function
```

VB_STAND.BAS

Functions used in processing the simple standard VB objects: list box, combo box, check box, and so on.

This BAS will be small but mighty. You'll use it every day and save a lot of code. We made a stab at some of these in the last chapter.

gfn_lst_finditem
gsb_form_center
gsb_set_chk

API.BAS

API calls are tedious to write. Create the API Declare statements and supporting routines in one or more common BAS files and save everyone else the headache.

Example:

```
Declare Function GetWindowsDirectory Lib "Kernel" (ByVal String,
    ⇨ByVal nSize As Integer)   As Integer
Declare Function GetSystemDirectory Lib "Kernel" (ByVal lpBuffer
    ⇨As String, ByVal nSize As Integer) As Integer


Function gfn_get_dir (as_type As String) As String

    Dim li_Size As Integer

    Dim ls_Buffer As String

    Dim li_ValidLength As Integer


    li_Size = 150

    ls_Buffer = Space$(li_Size)


    Select Case UCase(as_type)

        Case "WINDOWS"

            li_ValidLength = GetWindowsDirectory(ls_Buffer, li_Size)


        Case "SYSTEM"

            li_ValidLength = GetSystemDirectory(ls_Buffer, li_Size)


        Case Else

            MsgBox ("Invalid directory name passed to gfn_get_dir.")

            gfn_get_dir = ""

            Exit Function


    End Select
```

```
        gfn_get_dir = Left$(ls_Buffer, li_ValidLength)


    End Function
```

Do you really want to write that twice? We got everything we need right here: a case statement to handle two possibilities with room to grow, error trapping, argument prefixing, the works. Top of the world, ma. Top of the world.

MASK.BAS

Different masks used in the KeyPress event of a TextBox, used to allow only certain values:

gfn_mask_alpha_only
gfn_mask_numeric_only
gfn_mask_integer_only

Example of function call:

```
    Sub text_num_keypress(KeyAscii As Integer)

        KeyAscii = gfn_mask_numeric_only(KeyAscii)

    End Sub
```

See the section "The KeyPress Edit Check: A Madman Seeks Revenge" for additional info on this subject.

Care and Feeding of a VBX

There are a vast number of VBXs or Visual Basic Extensions available. These include VBXs that come packaged with VB and various third-party add-on products. They include such items as 3-D look controls, spreadsheets, text fields for specific data types, and many others. They add an enormous versatility to the VB environment. You can enhance the pleasure (and minimize the displeasure) of using a VBX by performing the following steps. I'll use a mythical SPRDSHET.VBX to illustrate the process.

Ask yourself why you need this VBX in the first place. Is it offering an advantage or feature not available in the standard control set, or is it just a pretty face? If you're already in the middle of developing a system, adding a new VBX introduces another potential problem to your existing mess. We added a spellchecker VBX to one of our applications. It works nice half the time. The other half of the time it crashes. I had to redo one of my own programs with standard controls after a fancy VBX kept failing. Also remember, this VBX must now be included in your installation procedure; if you don't, you're in for even more crashes.

With this in mind, don't assume that the control works as advertised. Make sure it performs as expected and doesn't screw up anything else. You want a VBX to act like a vanilla control when its not performing its special function, but that's not always the case. You're better off writing code in the **KeyPress** event of a normal text box to accept only numeric data than using a special numeric VBX that acts funny or causes unexpected General Protection Fault (GPF) errors. As with all computer products, be especially careful with version 1.0 releases. Some are real duds. To avoid unpleasant surprises, test the VBX thoroughly before including it in any applications. Find out all of his disgusting habits before he moves in for good.

Okay, we've determined that we really need a spreadsheet object, and it just came in. Don't go and throw it on everyone's PC. Put one person in charge of checking it out and giving the all clear sign. What should this person do? Test all the mundane actions with the VBX object (I'm not kidding—besides it won't take that long). Try the following tests (if they apply).

Look and Feel Test

Ask yourself:

★ Is the object's appearance consistent with your current control set? If not, is that okay?

★ What does the cursor look like inside the control? Does it deviate from the standard I-Beam? Is that going to be problem for the users?

★ Set the control's property Enabled = False. Does the object turn that familiar disabled gray? If not, is that okay?

Standard Processing Test

★ Assign and retrieve a value from the control.

★ Assign bad data. If the control accepts only certain data types or ranges of values (such as numerics, values between 1 and 10, and so on), then check that it doesn't result in a

GPF if an improper value is entered.

> Try the cut and paste method (Shift-Ins) to put unacceptable data in the control.

> Try assigning it a bad value from a programming statement.

```
txt_numeric.text = "aaa"
```

Getting an unexpected GPF during development is a wicked experience. You're cooked. You probably need to exit Windows, reenter, reload VB, reload the project, and start again. You still don't know what's wrong. You might spend all day GPFing until you track down the problem. This is why we do this test. If you know ahead of time that a control acts flaky in certain circumstances, you have an idea what to check when you get a GPF.

☆ Clear the current value in the control from code. If the object accepts only numeric data or has a specific data mask how do you clear it?

Can you clear it like a regular textbox control:

```
txt_numeric.text = ""
```

Sometimes you have to do a little dance to get these objects blank again.

☆ Does any process happen automatically in this object if a certain function key is pressed?

Example:
SPRDSHET clears a data cell when **F2** is pressed.

Determine if this will cause any conflicts with your existing applications. Say you already have a standard of using **F2** to save data (for whatever twisted reason). You must now tell the users that in this special case they must press **F2** to clear the field. Watch them hang you by your ribs from the nearest tree.

Specific Functionality Test

If the VBX survives these simple tests, then move on to a full test of specific functionality. Make sure it does whatever it's suppose to do. Besides testing the VBX, this helps you decide if it has enough merit to be included with the rest of the boys. If the VBX has survived our hazing, we can move on.

Now It's BAS File Time

If the VBX is anything complicated such as a spreadsheet, data grid, graph, or such, immediately create a BAS file for it. Use the VBX's file name as the name of the BAS file. Once completed, plan on moving this BAS file to a global area so that everyone can use it. Now you can really get the most out of the VBX.

First check the VBX documentation to see if it included a text or BAS file with constants that you can use. If so, it saved you some work. Put the constants in the declarations section of the BAS file you created. Otherwise, scan the manual to look for likely candidates for constants. Any list of properties or assignments that use numeric values are probably better written as constants in your code.

Example:

SPRDSHET.VBX has several data types: numerics = 1, alpha = 2, date = 3, and so on, which are assigned like this:

```
Spd_Main.ColDataType = number
```

That's prime constant material if I ever saw it.

In addition to using constants, see if you can make any of the standard processing into a generic routine call. The techniques for writing global routines all come in here. Pass the control in as an argument and you're on your way. One of the first things I did when I began VB development was make a generic GRID.BAS to use for processing the standard VB grid, and a data grid VBX add-on to use for retrieving SQL. I use these routines every day.

Very simple examples:

```
Sub gsb_grd_set_text(a_grd As Control, ai_row As Integer, ai_col
    ⇨As Integer, as_text As String)

    a_grd.row = ai_row

    a_grd.col = ai_col

    a_grd.text = as_text

End Sub


Function gfn_grd_get_text(a_grd As Control, ai_row As Integer,
    ⇨ai_col As Integer ) As String

    a_grd.row = ai_row

    a_grd.col = ai_col

    gfn_grd_get_text = Trim(a_grd.text)

End Function
```

Calling routine code example:

```
If gfn_grd_get_text(grd_employee, 1, 1) = "" Then

     Call gsb_grd_set_text(grd_employee, 1, 1, "Test")


End If
```

The calling routine's code is reduced considerably, especially if there are a lot of assignments. Why keep writing the same boring stuff over and over? The constants and routines in the BAS file can be added on as you gain more knowledge about the workings of the VBX. Also include any "gotchas" in the declaration section before the constants. That way the BAS file acts like a bulletin board. Share all the painful secrets you learned during the initial testing phase.

Putting all the supporting code for a VBX in one BAS file has several advantages:

☆ You don't need to add the BAS in projects that don't require this particular VBX. Projects and subsequent EXEs will not suffer from code bloat.

☆ It is a convenient and easy convention. If you are wondering if the processing has already been done for you, skim through the appropriate BAS file.

☆ VBXs often have properties and attributes that are not found in standard controls already in the project. These include the **Row** property in a grid or the **Action** property in a spreadsheet. If you put generic VBX code in a more standard BAS file, then programs might not compile unless you include the VBX in all projects that use it. You'll get "Property Not Found" error messages. Then you'll be forced to include the VBX in unnecessary projects just so you can compile your program.

Sample VBX Setup for a Mythical Spreadsheet Object
SPRDSHET.BAS (Declarations Section)

```
Option Explicit


'Naming Convention: spd_

'_____ General Information _____

'Warning - once in edit mode the KeyPress event is no longer triggered.

'No keystrokes can be trapped/converted

'Instead use the MASK property
```

```
'GPF Occurs If Numeric Type Cells Are Assigned Alpha Data
'spd_main.cell = 1
'spd_main.text = "aaa" - crashes if cell 1 is numeric datatype
'_____ End General Information _____
'_____ Constants _____


'Constants Used For The Action Property
Global Const SPD_GOTO = 1
Global Const SPD_CLEAR = 2


'Specific Data Types
Global Const SPD_NUM = 1
Global Const SPD_CHAR = 2
Global Const SPD_DATE = 3



'_____ End Constants _____
```

Routines included:

```
function gfn_spd_get_cell_data(a_spd As Control, ai_row As Integer,
    ⇨ai_col As Integer) As String


sub gsb_spd_set_cell_data(a_spd As Control, ai_row As Integer,
    ⇨ai_col As Integer, as_text As String)


sub gsb_spd_clear_all(a_spd As Control)
```

and so on. Now, I just made this thing up, but you see how useful this can be.

This imaginary code snippet is pretty readable even if you don't know what the VBX is.

```
spd_main.Action = SPD_CLEAR
If gfn_spd_get_cell_data(spd_main, 1, 1) <> "" Then
     Call gsb_spd_clear_all(spd_main)
     Call gsb_spd_set_cell_data(spd_main, 1, 1, "Eldon")
     Call gsb_spd_set_cell_data(spd_main, 1, 2, "Tyrell")
End If
```

```
spd_main.Cell = 1, 1

Spd_Main.ColDataType = SPD_NUM

spd_main.Action = SPD_GOTO
```

Long stretches of duplicate code can go away. The constants increase readability.

I don't use that many third-party VBXs in my current development; our database add-on, a spreadsheet, some masked data controls, and that's about it. A masked control, like a text box that allows only a valid date, might be a useful additional to your own collection. Probably the third-party VBX that you'd get the most use out of would be a spreadsheet. A spreadsheet acts as an editable grid. You can't directly edit fields in the standard VB grid. I've seen workarounds like having a floating text box that moves in front of the current cell of the grid, but that's really getting into serious voodoo programming. Besides, a spreadsheet usually supports data formatting and drop-down combo box fields that aren't available in the standard GRID.VBX. It's very useful for multiple record processing (Figure 2.1).

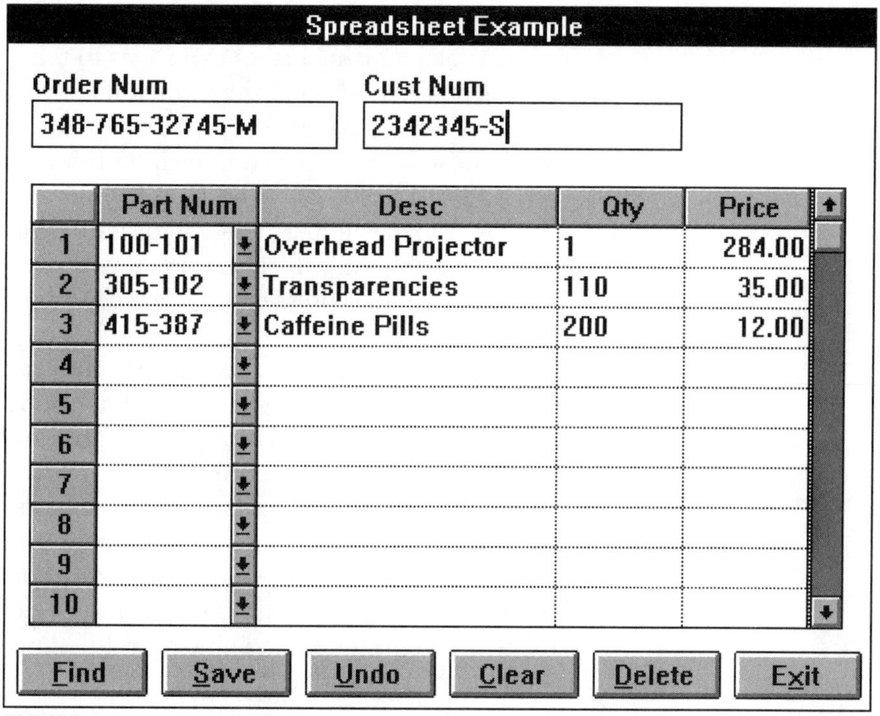

FIGURE 2.1 The spreadsheet allows the entry of multiple items.

In addition to the vast array of available VBXs, you can also create your own. The information is in the *VB Professional Features* manual. But, you better know C and/or C++. (I don't know either so at best I'm a wretched outcast in the programming world.) Unless you're just looking for a challenge, I'd recommend you find out whether there is an existing VBX out there already before you hit the C code. Let some other poor guy do the work for you. Believe me, there's already enough challenging stuff to do in a large application.

Global Forms: Uncommon Dialog Boxes

The VB manual has a rather weird chapter about creating custom common dialog boxes. A custom common dialog box is just a popup form, but that doesn't sound nearly as impressive. It really gets down in the dirt about setting the default button, control focus, and the form's properties. It even says how you can make a collection of them that can be used in many applications. I've read the chapter a couple of times now. While it tells you how to make one heck of a box, it doesn't really tell you how you're going to get information back and forth from these little guys.

That's the big issue, isn't it? Perhaps an example would have been in order. When a manual takes two pages to tell you to line up the buttons on the bottom of the form you know it has got something to hide. I think the idea that it's a generic form that supposedly can be called from any application really throws the writers. Even VB's own standard dialog boxes have problems. You have to set up an On Error Goto ErrHandler thingy in order to trap if the user hits the Cancel button. Sorry, I laugh every time I see that awful contraption. Since when is pressing the Cancel button an error?

The problem is that a form is not the same as a routine. A form isn't called; it's shown. A global function can be passed a whole slew of argument variables from the calling procedure and then return a value. That's what it was born to do. It is its destiny. However, you can't directly pass a variable to a form like you would with a subroutine. I remember early in our development when we realized this. We had plans for all these nice global forms that could be called to perform standard processing, and then realized, "Hey, wait a minute. The form doesn't know what I'm doing. Then I call it. Now I don't know what it just did. Uh oh."

This is the one fundamental problem when using a global form for processing. How do you pass information back and forth to this form? Either you use global variables or a load/set control value/show/get control value/unload process. These can be done either using in-line code or within a global function call. If you understand what I just said, then go on to the next chapter. My capacity to explain all this leaves much to be desired.

Global Channel Variables

One method is to use global variables reserved specifically for transporting data between the routines. The calling procedure assigns the global variable the original value or desired action, then launches the form. The form then checks the global variable and processes accordingly. Information is also returned using global variables.

Here's a simple example. More complicated form calls are done the same way. We need a popup form that has a large (254 MaxLength) text box for entering big comments (Figure 2.2). This form can be shown if a main form is tight on space and has no room to put a comment text box. A command button on the main form will pop it up displaying the current contents of the comment field. The text can be edited on this form. The form will have two command buttons: OK, and Cancel.

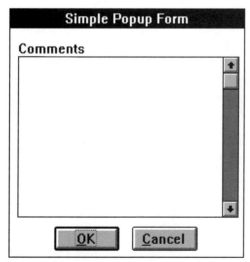

FIGURE 2.2 Global comments popup form.

The calling procedure would look something like this:

```
gs_channel_var = fs_COMMENTS              'Assign global variable the
    ⇨current comments
frm_popup_comments.Show MODAL             'Display the popup form


'Form is shown MODAL so this code is executed when the form
    ⇨is unloaded
Select Case gs_channel_result             'Comand button click event
    ⇨assigns this global


    Case "CANCEL"                         'Cancel command button
    ⇨pressed
        Exit Sub


    Case "OK"                             'OK command button pressed
        fs_COMMENTS = gs_channel_var      'Current comment assigned
            ⇨to gs_channel_var
        fi_changes_made = true


End Select
```

The code on the popup form:

```
Sub Form_Load
        txt_comments.text = gs_channel_var 'Assign textbox the
            ⇨global variable
End Sub


Sub cmb_ok_click
        gs_channel_result = "OK"            'Pass back that OK
            ⇨button was pressed
        gs_channel_var = txt_comments.text 'Pass back changed contents
        Unload Me
End Sub


Sub cmb_cancel_click
                                'Don't change global variable
        gs_channel_result = "CANCEL"        'Pass back that Cancel
            ⇨button was pressed
```

```
        Unload Me
    End Sub
```

That's pretty straightforward. The whole thing could be jazzed up quite a bit. Just understand how the globals allow us to pass both data and status information.

If the popup form displays retrieved data, then an SQL call might be passed to it and executed. The results might be displayed in a list box or grid. In cases like these, where multiple data values might need to be returned, arrays can be used to pass the information.

In my current development work, channel variables are used to transfer information back and forth. The most heavily used popup form is a data record finder (Figure 2.3). An SQL statement is passed via global variables. All the retrieved records are displayed in a data grid. The user selects the desired record, then presses the Select command button. All the field values in the selected record are passed back via a global array. These values can then be assigned to the calling form's controls for display and editing.

Types of information that might be passed to the form:
> Current data value to be displayed or selected.
> SQL statement to be executed; results displayed on the popup form.

Types of information that might be passed back from the form:
> The command button that was pressed on the form—Cancel, OK, Delete.
> One or more data values.
> Status of what happened—success/failure.

Popup Data Finder Form		
Title	**Year**	**ISBN**
Windows For Idiots	1990	1234567890
Windows For Morons	1989	2345678901
Windows For Imbeciles	1988	3456789012
Windows For Half-Wits	1987	4567890123
Windows For CIOs	1986	5678901234

Select   Cancel

FIGURE 2.3 Record finder popup form.

Global Channel Variables within a Function

We can convert the previous in-line code to a global function:

```
Function gfn_frm_comments(as_comments As String) As String

    gs_channel_var = as_comments          'Assign global to
        ⇨passed in argument

    frm_popup_comments.Show MODAL 'Show popup form

    gfn_frm_comments = gs_channel_result 'Function returns
        ⇨either 'CANCEL' or 'OK'

    as_comments = gs_channel_var          'Argument passed in is changed!

End Function
```

Calling procedure:

```
Select Case gfn_frm_comments(fs_COMMENTS)


    Case "OK"

        fi_changes_made = true


    Case "CANCEL"

        Exit Sub


End Select
```

This approach leaves less clutter in the calling procedure. We can hide the actual global variables by assigning their value to argument variables passed to the function. However, there is a problem here. If you wrote a routine like the one preceding for all your popup forms and put them all in a global BAS file, you would have to include all the popup forms in your project as well. Why? The routine uses the actual form name in the **Show** command. You'll get a "Variable not defined" error if you try to run without all the forms included. Oops. I don't want do that. We can put each calling routine in its own separate BAS file. That might not be a bad idea; or, we can fall back on our previous global routine training. That's right, we can pass a form into a routine as a variable.

```
Function gfn_frm_comments(a_frm As Form, as_comments As
    ⇨String) As String

    'Remember frm_popup_comments must be used as the a_frm
        ⇨argument!

    gs_channel_var = as_comments
```

```
                    a_frm.Show MODAL

                    gfn_frm_comments = gs_channel_result

                    as_comments = gs_channel_var

              End Function
```

Calling function:

```
              Select Case gfn_frm_comments(frm_popup_comments,
                 ⇨fs_COMMENTS)

                    'the rest is the same
```

I'm starting to like the one form, one BAS file idea. I prefer function calls to in-line code, and the global variables used in the form can be defined in the accompanying BAS file. No matter what you decide, just make sure the global variables for popup form processing are conspicuously named so that no one mistakenly makes an assignment to them.

No Global Variables Technique

The load form, assign control, show form, wait, hide form, get control value, unload form method (whew). I think the VB manual was alluding to this method. We use the **Load** and **Show** commands to do this. Here's the previous example without global variables.

```
              Load frm_popup_comments       'Form loaded into memory but
                                                ⇨not displayed

              frm_popup_comments.txt_comments.
                 ⇨text = fs_COMMENTS          'Assign value to control on
                                                ⇨the loaded form

                                             'Yes, you can do this even though
                                             'the form is not shown

              frm_popup_comments.Show MODAL  'Show the form and wait

              'This is executed after the popup form is hidden

              If frm_popup_comments.
                 ⇨ActiveControl.Caption =
                 ⇨"&OK" Then                 'Pressed the OK command button

                    fs_COMMENTS = frm_popup_comments.txt_comments.text

                                             'Assign the value in the textbox

                                             'Yes, you can do this too even
                                             'though the form is hidden

              End If

              Unload frm_popup_comments      'Unload form from memory
```

The code on the popup form:

```
Sub cmb_ok_click

        cmb_ok.SetFocus          'Needed because I set cmb_ok's property
                                    Default = true

        Me.Hide                  'Just hide, don't unload the form -
                                    controls can still be referenced

End Sub

Sub cmb_cancel_click

        cmb_cancel.SetFocus      'Needed because I set cmb_cancel's
                                    property Cancel= true

        Me.Hide                  'Just hide, don't unload the form -
                                    controls can still be referenced

End Sub
```

The reason we can use this technique is that once a form is loaded into memory using the **Load** command, we can start referencing its controls even though it isn't displayed. We can set a value in a text box, add items to a list box, or fill a grid. Additional setup information like an SQL statement can be passed to the form by assigning it to an invisible control or the form's Tag property.

Now we show the form. Code can be placed in the form's **Activate** event to perform any processing that is dependent on the values we just assigned to the form. It might use the text assigned to a hidden text box named **txt_SQL_call** to execute a query. In this No Global Variables Technique the command buttons don't unload the form; instead, the **Me.Hide** command is issued. The calling procedure can then get the value in a control on the popup form before unloading it. It can get the value in a text box, the selected item in a list box, or the current row in a grid, and use this information accordingly. The form can then be unloaded.

In this example, I used **frm_popup_comments.ActiveControl.-Caption** to figure out which button was pressed. Again, I'm guessing this is what the VB manual wanted me to do. The problem with doing this is that if you set the Default or Cancel property to True on the command buttons, then you aren't guaranteed that focus will return there when exiting the form. Pressing the Enter (Default) or the Esc (Cancel) key will trigger the button's click event without setting focus to the control itself. You need to include an explicit **SetFocus** command in the click event of the button to make sure the focus returns there. Again, any information like this could instead be assigned to an invisible control or the form's tag property and interrogated by the calling procedure.

```
Sub cmb_ok_click

    txt_button_pressed.text = "&OK"    'Instead of setfocus -
        ⇨assign action to a hidden control

    Me.Hide                            'Just hide, don't unload the
        ⇨form - controls can still be referenced

End Sub
```

Calling procedure:

```
If frm_popup_comments.txt_button_pressed.text ="&OK" Then

    'rest is the same
```

You get the point. There are a lot of ways to go here. Find something you're comfortable with.

We can again convert this to a function instead of using in-line code, but I think I've gone on too long already. I'm throwing out a lot of weird stuff here. Set up your own examples and practice. See what works best in your situation, but once you've decided on a method, stick with it. A few well-designed global popup forms can make your life a whole lot easier. Spend the time and do it right.

Standard Processing: Form Follows Data

Companies need computer applications for one main reason: Data. Applications must retrieve, display, update, save, delete, and report data. It's easy to forget this amidst all the wild API tricks, fancy 3-D buttons, and assorted bells and whistles. However, if your jazzy application doesn't perform data operations quickly, efficiently, and correctly it's junk, and believe me, the users will tell you so. The method you use to access data will be the biggest influence on your screen design and standard processing. Any screen design must take into account the limitations of the data access method.

The method and controls used to allow VB to talk to data vary between companies and platforms. The selection of an access method, whether it's VB's own Access data control or a third-party add-on, is a crucial decision that must be made before serious development begins.

These are the different ways to access data that I know are currently being used in development:

★ Flat files and standard VB file I/O: This is not the way to go for anything complicated. I actually wrote a short section later on, "Standard File I/O: Dragging a Brick with a String," just to tell you this.

★ Bounded Controls—look Ma, no code: Bounded controls are the easiest method if you can live with their limitations. This can be done using the Access control that comes as part of VB 3.0. Usually the method works something like this: A special data access control is set with the table name, location, and selection condition. A set of bounded controls is created to hold all the data fields that are to be displayed. Each bounded data control on the form is set to display a specific field. If you're lucky, you can bind the sexier controls like check boxes, option buttons, and combo boxes. Otherwise, you need to do double assignments—one to an invisible bounded control which then triggers (in the Change event) another assignment to the desired VB control. The same process must be reversed to get the data back into the bounded control.

The data set is retrieved, displaying one record at a time in the bounded controls. Usually there is a special command button or scroll bar that allows the user to run through the records. The specifics of inserting, updating, and deleting records are usually taken care of by command buttons. The user presses the Insert command button, types the record into the bounded data controls, and presses the Save command button. This may require no or only minimal coding. Provided you create the control set adhering to the strict setup rules, the data control performs all the insert/update/delete SQL calls for you.

This is a quick process. You can slap a program together rapidly if you're willing to follow along and process data exactly the way the whole bounded control set is expecting it. Of course, anything that is designed to make your life easier usually achieves it by limiting your options. Think of the whole bounded control paradigm as joining a cult. Do everything the way you're supposed to and everybody's happy. For the most part, application developers are a bit too unsociable to join cults, and tend to avoid bounded controls as well. I remember when I had to give a presentation to my development group explaining the strict, guided tour processing expected by our bounded control set. Those developers who didn't fall asleep at my somnolent delivery just rejected the whole thing and decided to use standard controls with raw SQL calls.

★ Dynaset: In a dynaset, data is retrieved into a memory grid. You can usually sweep through the data in a somewhat standard grid process, but the actual dynaset can't be viewed on the screen. The data must be copied to a regular grid or standard controls in order to be viewed and edited. VB's data control uses a dynaset underneath those bounded controls. As you scroll though the records using the data scroll bar, VB runs through the dynaset, copying the current record into the bounded controls. The dynaset is the brains behind the scheme. Inserts/updates/deletes are either performed by assigning values to the current record in the dynaset's memory or by issuing specific commands used by the dynaset to perform these operations. Otherwise a standard SQL call might be issued.

★ Data Grid: The data grid is not just a place in memory but an actual object that can be displayed on the screen. The grid can be scrolls and the values copied into standard controls for editing. Most likely you can't do any SQL inserts/updates/deletes directly on this data grid; instead, a standard SQL call is needed. In this case, the SQL call might be passed to another data object used in conjunction with the grid that can process and issue the statement.

To be honest, this is the way we do things in my current development, and it's really the only way I know. We rejected a set of third-party bounded controls. When we were starting out, VB's Access data control wasn't even invented yet. We got things working using this scheme and that's that. The last thing you want to do after you have a solid working relationship with a data access method (global routines, workarounds, standard processing, knowledge of quirks and limitations) is to start fishing around looking for new ways to do things.

The other developers I know all use some form of a dynaset to retrieve data (using ODBC) and standard SQL calls or stored procedures to process data. No matter which method you use to process data, most likely it's tedious, time-consuming, occasionally horrifying, and affects every other decision and action in your development.

Which Data Access Control/Method Is Right for You?

Questions to answer when considering a data access control/method:

- ☆ Does it support your current development platform? Can it talk to your data? Don't buy what you can't use.

- ☆ Can it execute an in-line SQL Select statement? How? How about SQL insert/update/delete statements? Can these SQL statements be used, or must changes to data come through assignments to bounded controls or to the dynaset in conjunction with commands specific to the data control?

- ☆ What kind of SQL can it execute? Standard or its own funky variation? How limited is this SQL? Can you do regular joins, outer joins, unions, nested selects? Can it execute a SQL stored procedure?

- ☆ How does it handle concurrence/data integrity?

- ☆ Does it support transaction processing? How?

- ☆ How robust is the product? How does it hold up when processing large amounts of data? The following info is absolutely vital. Don't just read the manual to find it, do a stress test:
    - Number of tables that can be included in a single SELECT statement.
    - Number of total records that can be retrieved.
    - Maximum number of columns that can be retrieved.
    - Maximum total size (sum of the column widths) of all columns retrieved.

    Are any of these values too low to support the processing in your application? Is the retrieval time of large data sets too slow?

- ☆ Can you live with its limitations? Can you code around them? Can the users live with resulting applications?

This is big deal stuff. Don't think I was considered to make such a decision. I just went along with what the big boys figured out. Most likely you'll have to do that too. Of course, if they make the wrong decision, you're the one who'll pay the price. Coding around the limitations of a data access method can take up most of your time.

Don't rely on word of mouth, a grinning salesperson, or a write-up in a computer magazine when making this decision. You have to get your hands on the actual product and put it thorough its paces. Don't just use the ridiculous examples that will be provided on the how-to diskette either. You need to design a small but comprehensive test application. This application will help you decide if this data access control is going to work and become the basis for determining which standard processing and screen design will be used in later applications. Once again, probably some big cheese will be conscripted into this assignment.

Following is a list of standard processes that most applications must perform, written in my best attempt at pseudocode. I've made some suggestions for what should happen during each process. As always, they are suggestions, not commandments. I just want you to think about how you want your application to handle each standard process. Once you've written your sample application, it can stand as a foundation for all further development work. Working on this sample application will be an integral part of your initial project startup.

Through its development you'll begin to determine:

☆ Necessary global routines.

☆ Global popup forms and what information must be communicated between them and the main form.

☆ Standard message boxes to be included in your equivalent of MSGBOX.BAS.

☆ Coding techniques and routines to handle standard processing.

☆ The general format of your screen design.

Startup Processing

Usually performed on a login form
User must enter correct name and password to enter the application
Usually performed on a login form, main form, or the startup routine Sub Main().
> read INI file and assign any contingent global variables
> connect to the server and database
> check user rights to enter specific application/processing

If the user has sufficient rights then
> display selected form/desired application

Load Data or Find Record Processing (Same Thing, Two Names)

If currently editing a record check if any changes have been made
     If changes have been made then
         Display Message ("Save changes to current record?")
         with options:
             1) Yes - perform Save Processing
                If successful save then Load Processing
             2) No - perform Load Processing
             3) Cancel - just return to the form

Perform Load Processing

The actual load process will vary greatly depending on your data access control. Some applications (mainly using bounded controls as seen in Figure 2.4) have a simple retrieve process that just throws up a current record. The user flips through the records serially or jumps around with a scroll bar. I can't imagine a user would want to do this, especially if there is a lot of data.

Some applications allow the user to fill in one or more of the edit fields and then press the **Find** command button to look for a match. A variation on this is to check for a match on the **lostfocus** event of the key field, loading an existing record if there is a match. If the table allows duplicates of the field used in this match, the user must have the option to edit the existing record or add a new one.

The preceding methods don't give the user a tabular view of the records. Users generally want more of a grid-like device for viewing all possible records and then selecting the desired entry. A data grid can be displayed on the form that lists the records available (Figure 2.5). The user selects a record from the grid with a click or double-click, which copies it to standard controls for further processing. This satisfies the need for a tabular view of the data, but can take up screen space. This method gives the user the most information on

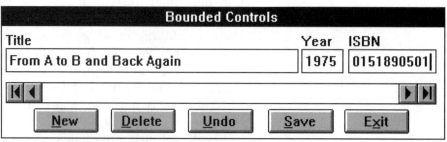

FIGURE 2.4 Bounded control set.

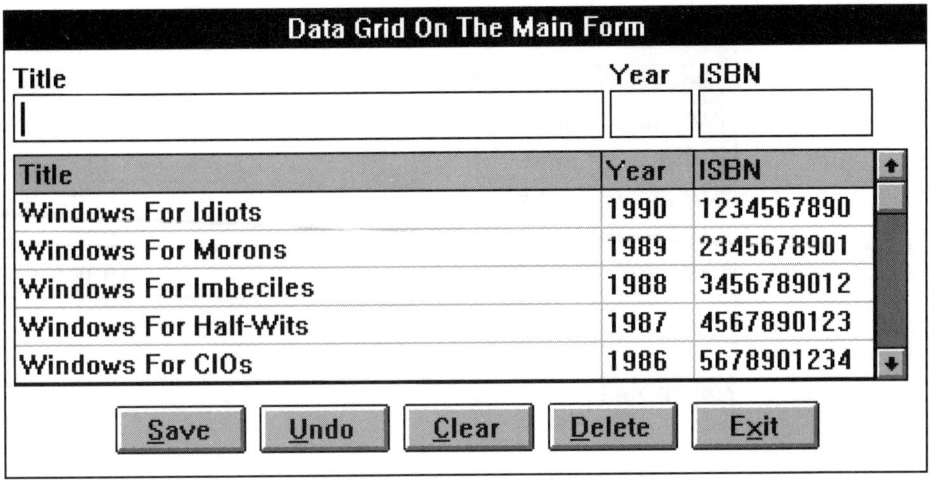

FIGURE 2.5 Data grid on the main form.

screen, but as forms become more complicated and filled with controls, you'll have to shrink your data grid to conserve space. A scrollable data grid that is only two records high is a pitiful sight. Our development group originally used this method until it was determined that the considerable loss of screen space wasn't worth the warm and fuzzy feeling the users got from seeing all the data right there on the form. I remember there was quite a little battle over this.

The other alternative is a data grid on a separate global popup form. When the **Find** command button or menu item is clicked this popup form is launched (Figure 2.6). An SQL statement is passed to this popup form and executed. The results are displayed in the data grid. The user scrolls thorough this grid and selects the desired record. The unique key field or all the data fields are returned to the calling form. The data values are then copied into standard controls for editing. If only the unique key field is passed back, then an additional SQL call must be made to get the additional field values. Many bells and whistles can be added to this global popup form that allow searches through the grid based on specific fields and values, pattern matches, and so on.

Save Processing

Check for missing required fields
If not filled in then
> *Display Message* ("Required field(s) missing. Please enter: " + list fields)

Check for any other special things specific to the application (uniqueness, range checking, rights to save, etc.)

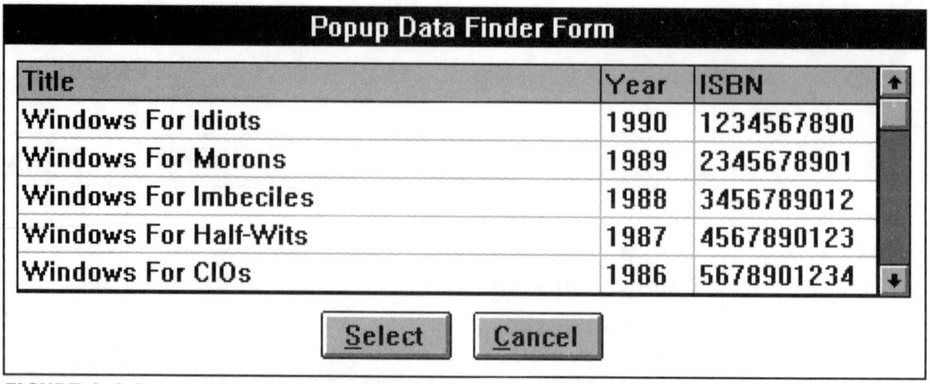

Popup Data Finder Form		
Title	**Year**	**ISBN**
Windows For Idiots	1990	1234567890
Windows For Morons	1989	2345678901
Windows For Imbeciles	1988	3456789012
Windows For Half-Wits	1987	4567890123
Windows For CIOs	1986	5678901234

Select   Cancel

FIGURE 2.6 Record finder popup form.

If not correct in then
> *Display Message* ("Special things aren't done: " + list fields or problems)

If editing old record
> Check if any changes made to the record
> If no changes then
>> *Display Message* ("No changes have been made.")

If saving a new record then
> Call to the function that generates the unique value for ID field in the record

Issue SQL statement/stored proc/dynaset assignment to save record(s)

If successful save then
> *Display Message* ("Save successful.")
> Perform Clear Processing

Else
> *Display Message* ("Save failed: " + reason why)

Undo Processing

Undo all changes to current record since last save
Reset any flag and hold variables, set focus back to the first control in the tab order

Clear Processing

Clear all data fields, reset any flag and hold variables, set focus back to the first control in the tab order

Delete Processing

Display Message ("Delete the current record?")
> With options:
>> 1) Yes - Delete current record
>>> Issue SQL statement/stored proc/dynaset assignment to

delete record(s)
If successful
Display Message ("Delete successful.")
Perform Clear Processing
Else
Display Message ("Delete failed: " + reason why)
2) No - cancel process, return to form

Physical deletes of data are a big deal. Always put up a message to confirm deletes.

Exit Processing

Has the user made any unsaved changes to data?
Yes
Display Message ("Data has been changed. Save record before exiting?") with options:
1) Yes   - save data, if successful then exit
2) No   - exit without saving data
3) Cancel - return back to form
No
Display Message ("Exit the application?") with options:
1) Yes   - exit
2) No   - return to form

Juggling Processes

Decide if you want an "Exit the application?" message on all forms. If you put it in, users will complain that they have to answer this stupid question. "I wouldn't have pressed the Exit button if I didn't want to exit," they'll sniff. If you don't put it in, the users will complain that they pressed the Exit button by accident and didn't really mean it. You won't win either way, but at least be consistent.

Remember, any edit checks performed at the regular save processing must also be performed at the "save then exit" and the "save then load new data." If the record fails any of the criteria needed to save, then you should not continue with the processing. Put up the warning messages and stop. Don't exit, don't load the new data. This will probably require a status flag variable. I've seen some applications really screw this up. This is a subtle thing that few people remember to test. I pointed out this problem in a number of programs written by our group and the mood turned quite savage.

Decide on a standard screen presentation for all the processes just mentioned. They can be called from command buttons or menu items. Decide which of these methods will be used. In my experience, users, especially new ones, prefer command buttons. Using just menu items will save screen space. You can use both menu items and command buttons, but please don't write the code in both locations. Have the menu item call the command button:

```
Sub mnu_exit_click

        Call cmb_exit_click

End Sub
```

Duplicating a process on both a command button and menu item requires some extra care. If you dis/enable one, you must dis/enable the other. If the Delete command button is disabled, but the Delete menu item is still enabled you've got a bug that might grant an unscrupulous user rights they really don't have.

Decide on a standard location and order for the command buttons or menu items on the form. Since this will be the bulk of most standard processing, it is important that each item appear in a consistent place. Don't surprise the users each time they enter a new form. Command buttons should not snake down the right side on one form, scroll across the bottom on another, and hug the top on yet another form. In addition to being in standard locations, the names of the processing should be consistent. Decide on one name — such as Load or Find, Delete or Remove, Exit or Quit — and stick to it.

I reemphasize that the previous standard processing pseudocode was only an example of one possible method. After you've read through it, rip the pages out of the book and burn them. Work through each of these processes fully on your own. Allow all members of the development group to comment and find any flaws in the design. This will be one hair-pulling time, I can assure you.

Early in my own development work I decided to also standardize the code location of these processes in all my programs. The following routines exist on all my forms:

function ffn_check_if_changes
function ffn_check_required_fields
function ffn_save_data
sub fsb_clear
and so forth . . .

I've used these same form-level routine names in every application I've done. I don't vary the names, nor do I sometimes place the code behind the button or menu item instead. The standard processing code is always in the same place. I go into one written three years ago, and I waste no time trying to find out the where or what I'm looking for. This is not the place to be creative.

I also suggest that whenever possible you base your standard processing on existing code. After developing a few programs, you'll see that much of it is quite similar. Cut and paste from the old application, then modify as necessary. Your routines will all have the same names, the code will look and act the same, and you'll be a happy-go-lucky, petty-little-details-obsessed guy like me. A whole wide world filled with Mark Warhols. Maybe it's best not to think about that too much.

The Global Variable: Pathway to Exotic Data Locales

Never hardcode the directory path, server, or database name from where your program accesses data. All life is transitory, especially data locations. Data is vital, location is not. You don't want to hunt though endless projects changing "c:\data\sys1\" to "c:\data\sys2\." I sat patiently for over half an hour watching someone do this when they installed a system they had written on one server onto another — "f:\userworks\time\data\" changed to "h:\timecard\data." Then everything needed to be recompiled. Then it didn't work anyway. Don't fall into this trap.

I tested a major application that had to exist in a directory with a specific name. The main directory name was hardcoded throughout this entire enormous project. If you had two versions on the same network drive, you had to run weird directory-renaming batch files before running different versions. Honest.

The best method is to have the program read a variable from an INI file to get the data location and then set it to a global variable. This global is used throughout the project instead of the evil hardcode.

Ugmo:

```
"f:\userworks\time\data\timecard.dbf"
'Used all over the place
```

Beauty:

```
Global gs_database As String

read INI file at startup, assign gs_database = "f:\userworks\time\data\"

gs_database + "timecard.dbf"      'Used all over the place
```

Although the data may travel a thousand miles, you need only change the INI file to keep up. You don't even need to recompile the projects. I've lived through the alternative. It's not a trip worth taking.

Odd Oaths in Design Review

The following standard processing and design issues emerged during the application design review cycle in my company. Application design review is a form of corporate hazing during which your work is reviewed, deconstructed, destructed, and handed back for a rewrite. Consider the pitfalls of any of these ideas if they are suggested during your own review cycle.

1. Adding an elaborate system to disable command buttons (or other controls) when not active.
   Problem: Requires trapping keypress events for each object, looping through checking their status, and so on.

It is not worth it.

Typical Examples:

☆ The **Undo** command button is disabled until a change made, then disabled again if all the fields are put back to original state (Figure 2.7). What a way to add overhead.

☆ The **Clear** command button is disabled until some data is entered into the edit fields. The radical fringe put up a mes-

Disabled Buttons					
Title		Year	ISBN		
Find	Save	Undo	Clear	Delete	E**x**it

FIGURE 2.7 Disabled Buttons.

sage box telling the users they can't clear because all fields are blank to begin with. I've actually seen the message box shown in Figure 2.8. What overkill. It's worse when you get a whole group of people in a room deciding this stuff who have no idea how much extra gunk this is going to add to everything in the system. Even the simplest applications can be made extraordinarily complicated with no real benefit to the user.

☆ The **Save** command button is disabled until all the required fields are filled in. This one requires our special attention. If you can't save because some conditions aren't met (like missing required fields), put up a message box when the Save button is pressed; don't disable it because users don't know what they have to do to get the button enabled again.

The ideal process at save is to put up a single message box listing all the missing required fields, then set focus to the first field in the list. Now I hate overhead but I think it's worth it in this case. To aid in this process, it's best to somehow designate required fields visually

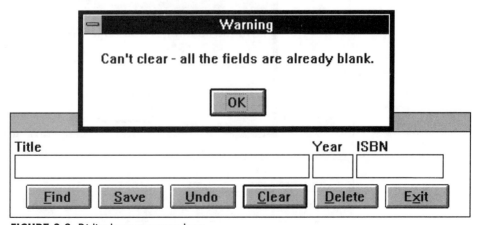

FIGURE 2.8 Ridiculous message box.

on the screen (Figure 2.9). In my current development, we set the property **FontUnderline = True** in the label accompanying the data field. It's unobtrusive but helpful. Decide on your own method (underline, color change, * or Rq appended to the text in the label) and then don't vary.

2. Reloading combo boxes with static lookup data after every save event: Unless your system really needs up the second information, just load any data objects at the Load event of the form. I knew one person who was obsessed with refreshing controls like the combo boxes displaying the State and Country fields every time an event was processed on the form. Now, when was the last time we added a new state?

3. Sudden shifts in methodology because someone read something in a computer "rag": As soon as you hear the phrase, "I was reading one of the rags just the other day," scream and run out of the room. Hopefully everyone else will join you. Carefully consider any new control set or change to standard processing or screen design. Don't make snap decisions based on any articles or product reviews. Standard processing in an application may indeed need to be changed after the initial protoyping phase, but these changes should be the result of your own careful assessments not on childish whims. Sudden changes in methodology can include a "painless" shift of all applications to an MDI Parent-Child

FIGURE 2.9 User presses the Save command button with missing required fields.

Interface because it looks so swell. Our group tried this and it almost killed me.

4. Breaking up existing processing over multiple forms: There is no greater torture than taking an existing application and distributing the existing processing over additional forms. Breaking up the swinging party on one form and scattering it into several subforms can be one wicked programming assignment. Later on, if it's decided that everything really looked better on one form, the agony will begin all over again.

5. Disco windows: One of the developers in my group used this term to describe applications that conditionally switch controls visible and invisible. The result is a strobe-like effect and constantly shifting control locations that can confuse users. Disco doesn't really bother me. It bothered me more when they made me rewrite my Disco Windows application to an MDI Parent-Child. It looked a lot better, but it was agony to code.

   If people are really complaining, see if you can disable the controls instead of making them invisible. This is less distracting. Another technique is to group the controls then move them into frames. Then the whole frame can be set in/visible. This is less flashy and helps emphasize the group identity of each control set. When all else fails, you might need to separate the controls onto different subforms. That's going to be a lot of work if you already have the program up and running.

6. Add/Edit/View/Delete/Report Orientation: Some applications divvy up the processing more than necessary. I have seen several applications in review that had a main screen that branched off into four or more subforms (Figure 2.10). New records were added on one form; editing old records was done on another. There was a separate form to view records and another to delete them. You want a report? It's on another form. You don't want your users to have to seesaw back and forth like this. The user should be able to perform all these actions on just one form. If your system has

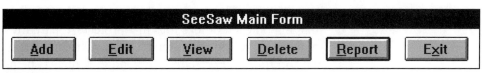

FIGURE 2.10 SeeSaw Main Form.

security based on the Add/View/Edit/Delete/Report model, then just put up a message box stating that the user doesn't have rights to perform the requested action or disable the command button or menu item.

Overall Application Setup: Dodge City

One question that I'm always asked by people who are planning to begin VB development is how on earth can they develop a large application that requires the effort of many programmers. I don't think they believe it can be done. But it is done, every day, by sad sacks like me. The biggest concern people have is how to keep from stepping on each other's toes in a project. Apparently everyone wants a source code maintenance facility that provides version control and the ability to check out and lock objects being used so other people can't change them. They want a fancy CASE tool that will prevent any contentious behavior. By now there's probably an add-on product that will do this, but as it stands, there is no inherent code management function in VB 3.0.

Yup, we've got the wild west here. If both you and another developer are on different computers, both editing the same form or BAS file, then you're going to have a good old VB shoot 'em up. But unlike a gun fight, it's the guy who's slow on the draw who gets the tin star and the saloon girl with the heart of gold. When you load a project into VB, the files appear frozen in time to you. What you're looking at is a copy of the file in memory, not the real McCoy. You will not see any updates to code or objects performed by other programmers once you've loaded the file. If there are any changes — say a bug fix to a routine in a global BAS file — you must remove, then reload the file. Although you may be looking at an old copy, when you save, it's your version that becomes the new file.

Here's the 12:00 showdown: Dead-Eye Pete vs. Desperado Mark

Pete and Mark both load the same project into memory, including PRINT.BAS which contains complicated routines used to print generic reports.

Mark now leaves his post on a fruitless search for the previously mentioned saloon girl.

Pete codes up a storm in PRINT.BAS, rounding up bugs, mending fences, adding new routines. He saves his extensive work and moves on.

Mark returns, rejected, alone but for tumbleweeds and piped-in harmonica Muzak. He pops open PRINT.BAS and grimly types a single comment line:

```
'I'm a nice guy, why don't girls like me?
```

then saves the file.

In this one desperate act, all of Pete's new code is gunned down. The file is back to the way it was when Mark loaded it early this morning.

Dead-Eye Pete. Shot from behind and he never saw it coming. If Pete's still twitching, Mark better high-tail it out of town.

Now I haven't done this to my boss yet but this scenario is certainly possible. Remember this example when you read about data concurrency in the SQL chapter. The one thing that's on your side in VB is when you perform a Save Project — only those files that actually have be changed are updated. In the preceding example, if I had instead written my plaintive cry in the **Form_Load** event of EMPRPT.FRM, there'd be no harm done. That leads to the pivotal question, "What does VB consider a change?" You can scroll through and examine a BAS file without causing it to be resaved, but once you've typed anything, you've marked that file as changed and VB will try to save it again. That comment line was the killer. A single keystroke is enough; pressing Ctrl-Z to undo it won't help. This applies to both forms and BAS files. Forms have an additional trigger. VB saves the current screen location of loaded forms. If you move the form from its current position, then it's a marked man.

I spent a lot of time writing about putting routines in global BAS files, using global popup forms, and creating a template form for screen design. If by some stroke of luck I've made any sense, you might start creating your own global files. These files will constitute a large investment of time and effort and should be protected like a gold map. While we can't rely on VB to protect them, we can provide some form of protection. First of all, I suggest you put the global files in a separate directory from the rest of your VB projects.

I've mapped out two independent systems, EMP_SYS and INV_SYS, that both use global routines taken from the VB_GBLS directory. One immediate suggestion I have for any development group is that if you are developing on the network, then have all the programmers use the same drive letter to map to the development area. Otherwise, any explicitly mapped files in the project's MAK file won't get loaded if another developer attempts to load the project.

In the next example, all the VB development is done on the N: network drive. Let's say that Pete instead maps the network drive to O: and I have to take over his projects now that he's pushing up daisies. I'm going to have to figure out his old mapping by looking at the MAK file then try to reload the files in the project that VB couldn't find. Depending on the number of projects, this could be a real pain. Start out on the same path and all is well.

Here's what a sample directory structure in a development drive might look like:

```
N:\VB_GBLS\{Main directory for VB global files}
N:\VB_GBLS\BAS
```

```
N:\VB_GBLS\FRM

N:\VB_GBLS \TEMPLATE


N:\EMP_SYS\{Main directory for an Employee System}

N:\EMP_SYS\EMPIMP\{subsystem of the Employee System}

N:\EMP_SYS\EMPRPT\

N:\FMP_SYS\EMPSEC\

   . . .


N:\INV_SYS\{Main directory for an Inventory System

N:\INV_SYS\INVORD\{subsystem of the Inventory System}

N:\INV_SYS\INVPUR\

N:\INV_SYS\INVREQ\

   . . .
```

Each new system will have its own main directory. This is standard hard drive management stuff. The global files are off in their own main directory, possibly further subdivided into subdirectories based on function or file type. These global files are loaded into the applications as necessary. The programmers will typically have full rights to the application directories they are working on.

To protect the global files from being altered accidentally, either use the DOS command **ATTRIB** *filename* +r to set the files to read-only. Otherwise, use whatever security rights masking is inherent in your network to safeguard the global files by preventing the programmers from writing to the global directories. In my current development, we just set the files to read-only with the **ATTRIB** command. No, this isn't an iron safe. Someone can just reset the file status and make a mess, but hopefully you're not working with renegades. This is really just a safeguard against accidents. If I mistakenly tinker with a global routine, I can't post the change. Instead I get a message telling me I can't save since it's a read-only file. If you are indeed working with renegades, then use the network's security to prevent file tampering.

Any changes that need to be made in a global file are performed by a single individual, usually the project leader, who has been given responsibility for maintaining it. Any new ideas, enhancements, or bug fixes to this file are submitted to this person who must use his or her infinite wisdom to determine the appropriate course of action. If global routines and forms are carefully designed and

FIGURE 2.11 Login form.

tested, then this won't be a daily event. Most of the global files in my current development haven't been changed in a long time.

We now have the background needed for setting up an application:
1. The cautionary tale of Dead-Eye Pete (awareness of the danger of overwriting files).
2. Programmers using the same drive mappings.
3. Separation of global files and applications.
4. Read-only status for global files to prevent 1).

With these elements in mind, let's look at the application setup methods. I know of three ways of setting up a large VB application that are currently being used in development. Decide which of these is most appropriate for your application and environment or strike out on your own.

With each of these development methods the final application usually starts with a login form that requires a user name and password (Figure 2.11). If the user gets this info right, the login form gives way to a main system form (Figure 2.12). This is usually a big, hulking beast with a little brain. It might have a cool logo on it. This

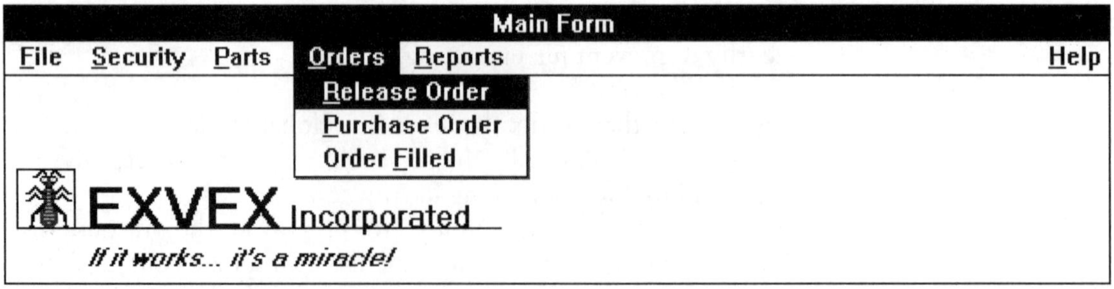

FIGURE 2.12 Main Application Form.

form calls the other separate processes either from command buttons or menu items.

Den of Thieves : One Single Project

This is certainly the most popular method for small, single-person development. A single project contains all the forms and BAS files in the application. This method is also used (which surprised me) for large applications with multiple programmers. Each programmer is assigned to one or more forms and BAS files in the project. Using these files the programmers work on their individual development tasks. It is imperative that no two programmers are responsible for the same file. Any necessary global files are included in the project and are used by all. A single executable file is created when development is complete.

Advantages:
1. Ideal for a single person developing a small, unified project.
2. Any global variables set are available to all forms and BAS files.
3. There is one single executable file.

Disadvantages:
1. Possibility of accidental overwrites. If you are using this method with multiple programmers, I would make it a practice to always use the Save File option instead of Save Project.
2. Possibility of having two programmers inadvertently use the same routine or global variable name on their individual BAS files. This is examined more in the second setup method.
3. Just how big and unwieldy is this project going to get? You might max out on forms or objects, the project might be to cavernous to navigate, or the final EXE might be too big to run.

The Roundup:
Separate Projects, One EXE

Here the processes are broken down into separate projects. The main shell project contains just the login and main form. After the programmers have finished their separate development, the individual files are loaded into this shell from the individual projects, then a single executable file is created. Since each standalone project

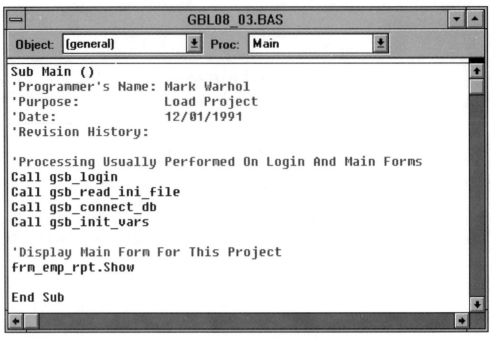

FIGURE 2.13 Sub Main() example.

doesn't include the main shell form, it has an additional BAS file with a Sub Main() routine (Figure 2.13). This is then set as the startup routine from the project's menu item Options-Project-Start Up Form. Sub Main() contains any login and initialization processing normally performed on the login and master forms. This BAS file isn't loaded into the final shell project.

Advantages:
1. Each programmer works in and is responsible for a separate project. Two programmers are never in the same place at the same time, so the overwriting of files is prevented. All projects still access the read-only global files.
2. Each separate project is more manageable and takes less time to load. The programmer doesn't have to wade through countless forms and BAS files that are irrelevant to the task at hand.
3. The benefit of having a single EXE application and shared global variables.

Disadvantages:
1. Big headaches are possible in the final roundup. In this scheme you must be especially careful about duplicate file

names. You must guard against programmers creating routines in separate BAS files that have duplicate names. VB will not allow two BAS files to have a nonprivate routine with identical names. Consider incorporating the BAS file name as part of all routines.

Example:

```
EMPRPT.BAS {includes}

    Sub gsb_EMPRPT_save_data

    Function gfn_EMPRPT_get_value


EMPSEC.BAS {includes}

    Sub gsb_EMPSEC_save_data

    Function gfn_EMPSEC_get_value
```

This naming convention might also be used for any global variables declared in these separate BAS files.

Example:

```
EMPRPT.BAS {includes}

    Global gi_EMPRPT_changes_made As Integer


EMPSEC.BAS {includes}

    Global gi_EMPSEC_changes_made As Integer
```

Likewise, all form names must be unique. Everyone can't use the name **frm_main** or again they won't load. The same rules apply in the previous setup method, but there the errors are handled on a daily basis, not all at once at the final load. In either method, consistent and fully explicit naming conventions are of primary importance to minimize these side-effect naming hazards. You don't want to devote a part of each day to chasing down and changing duplicate names.

2. Any bugs that result from interaction between the separate processes won't be found until this final executable file is created.
3. You must keep track of which files need to be loaded from each project.
4. The same problem as in the first method. How big is too big?

This Town Isn't Big Enough for the Two of Us: Separate Projects, Separate EXEs

Here the separate projects are not gathered together to create a single EXE. Instead, each project creates its own separate executable file. The main executable file actually runs the individual process EXEs, usually with the **Shell** command or the API call **WinExec**.

Advantages:
1. Each project and executable file is kept to a reasonable size. Very large applications cannot hope to run using just a single executable file. The file itself will be too large to run or there will be memory problems within the system.
2. Each programmer is responsible for a standalone project. There are no problems with overwriting files or duplicate variable or routine names. This is the easiest way to assign programming tasks without contention problems. An application of discrete projects devoted to separate processes can be easier to work with than one monster project with hundreds of files.

Disadvantages:
1. There is a loss of cohesiveness that results from not having a single executable file.

When the main EXE runs another EXE, it doesn't know what this program is doing or if it has ended. A global variable set in one EXE doesn't get set in the others. Such information must be communicated by some form of data exchange, possibly copying the information back and forth through the clipboard, a DDE link, or writing and reading from an INI file.

I have worked to some capacity with all of these setups. The first is used only for small utility programs that have just a form or two and aren't part of an interconnected system. Our group attempted the second method but then there was the MDI problem. There can only be a single MDI parent form in an application. The workaround to use a single MDI parent form through multiple applications was so hairy that eventually the whole idea was abandoned. Now any large-scale system is designed from the get-go as a combination of separate EXES that are launched from a main EXE. Our largest current system wouldn't work as a single executable. Maybe VB could load all the files and Windows could run the EXE, but nobody could handle maintaining such an hombre.

GRAPHICAL USER INTERFACE (GUI) DESIGN

The form is the face of your application. All your brilliant code will always remain hidden behind it. Good form design can't rescue a program that fails to save data, crashes on text searches, or runs like a tree sloth. It is, however, the key to user acceptance of a system. The application's appearance immediately gives the user clues about its quality. If it's done consistently and carefully, the users will have confidence in the system.

Bad form design makes users wary of the application. If it's ugly and confusing on the surface, they don't care what it does behind the scenes. They won't stick with it long enough to find out. If an application lacks a standard look and feel, it gives the impression that it was slapped together.

A well-designed product does not obscure the function it is trying to perform. Ideally, after the initial learning phase, the users shouldn't even notice your application anymore. You read that right; the application itself falls away. What is left is the process itself. The users aren't interested in your program (sorry I have to break that to you); they're interested in getting their work done.

You don't want to use a can opener. You want to eat a bowl of soup. If your opener is designed properly, you won't even remember opening the can because that's not your real goal. Design the opener incorrectly (I have one of these), and the user stops cold. "What is this thing? How does it go on the lid? Boy, this is awfully hard to use." Now it's the product, not the process that's getting the attention, and that's not where the focus belongs.

The most common form design issues are mentioned in the following sections. Establish design standards early, and you'll prevent most of the glaring errors. Remember our noble goal: an application that fades into obscurity.

Dress Blue : The Template Form

I created the following technique because setting up a new project was always such a chore. In the beginning, I manually set each form and control to our application standard one by one. But I always forgot something, and any inconsistencies were crucified in design review. "That not our standard!" the review team would bark in unison. I remember a particular incident when I used a rounded rectangle instead of a standard frame and threw the room into chaos. Where did that awful thing come from? Why did I use it? What was I thinking? Of course I didn't really tell them what I was thinking, opting instead to keep my job. It is with that incident still burning in my mind that I present this simple but effective time- and face-saver.

All your applications should give the impression of consistency. The way to achieve this visually is by using a template form for all your development work. You essentially design a uniform that all your applications are going to wear. Creating a template form as an intrinsic part of your development process early (not as a furtive time-saving gesture like mine) helps force you to think about your standard screen design and layout. Default colors, fonts, and controls are established here instead of letting everyone go off and do his or her own little scene. Trying to hunt down inconsistencies in screen presentation later in a project can be a big, boring chore. One project leader I spoke to says he goes into applications during off-hours and tries to set the properties to a consistent standard since the programmers just do whatever makes them feel good. My current development has well over a hundred separate projects spread out over multiple applications. Personally, I'm never in the mood to go hopping around resetting text box fonts.

Here's the trick to prevent the hopping. Create a standard shell project that will be used as a starting point for all future development work. It should include one or more standard template forms you define. Also include any global BAS files needed for standard techniques and any VB or third-party VBX controls typically used in your development: date objects, data grids, and so on. Including these files makes your template as close to a true application as possible.

Let's look at the some of the specific properties to set and controls to include on your template form.

Important Form Level Properties to Consider

- ☆ **BackColor**: The most important. The form should be set to the standard determined for all your applications. (See the section "Psychedelic Forms" for additional info.)

- ☆ **Icon**: If you have designed a standard icon for all your applications, then set it here. Anything is better than the lame VB default icons.

- ☆ **KeyPreview**: Set =True if all your applications need to trap and disregard keystrokes at the form level.

- ☆ **BorderStyle, ControlBox, MinButton, MaxButton**: Consider the following defaults, especially with a new-to-Windows user community:

☆ **BorderStyle**: Set at Fixed Single or Fixed Double instead of the VB default Sizable. It's best if forms are sized appropriately at design time. Users will accidentally shrink the window when trying to move it, obscure important fields or command buttons, then panic.

☆ **ControlBox**: Set to False. New users click this for no reason with alarming regularity. Its list of stark options then intimidates them. If you leave this enabled, make sure any exit processing you might have in an Exit command button gets called in the Form's Unload event. The ControlBox on a MDI Parent form cannot be set to false within Visual Basic. The API calls **GetSystemMenu** and **ModifyMenu** are needed to do this.

☆ **MinButton**: Set to False if the form is used as a modal popup. Users may try to avoid the modality by minimizing the form. They will then helplessly click around the inactive form that called the popup and wonder why it keeps beeping at them. Expect a bizarre call to the help desk.

☆ **MaxButton**: Set to False unless there's a hidden treasure waiting when the form opens wide. The maximized form will obscure the workplace and again confuse the user.

Controls and Properties

The standard form should have one of every object that a typical form might include.

Example:
>check box
>label
>text box
>grid
>combo box

Set the **Name** Property of each control to the standard prefix your development group decided on during your naming conventions meeting. This helps reinforce any written standard you might have.

Example:
>check box: chk_
>label: lbl_
>text box: txt_

Explicitly set **FontName**, **FontSize**, **BackColor**, and **ForeColor** for all objects on the form. (Read the section "Psychedelic Forms" for more on why.) Don't vary between fonts and colors.

I discussed standard processing in "Standard Processing: Form Follows Data." This form should include any command buttons used for these processes. Align them in the predetermined order and screen location you decided on in your standard processing meeting.

Example:

Find, Save, Undo, Clear, Delete and Exit command buttons aligned across the form, either along the bottom or in a button bar at the top.

Decide if any of these command buttons will have the **Cancel** or **Default** property set to True. Users will notice any inconsistencies and will want to know why **Esc** doesn't works on all the forms.

"Which forms?" you'll ask.
"I dunno. It seems sometimes it works, sometimes it doesn't. I forget where. It's annoying."

Believe me, you won't have time later on to tracking down things like this.

Include any default menu items in standard locations and with appropriate access keys. If your goal is to meet CUA interface standards, then set it up here. Programmers can easily delete unnecessary menu options when creating a new project.

&File	&Edit	&Put Additional Options Here	&Help
&New	&Undo		
&Open	Cu&t		
&Save	&Copy		
Save &As	&Paste		
&Print	Cl&ear		
E&xit	&Delete		

The template form can also include calls to startup global routines or standard code performed in all applications; login to the database, center the form on the screen, setting the help option to the right corner of the form, and so on. The Form_Load event is the most likely place to put these. You could also make empty shell routines on the form that would later contain standard processing code, such as:

```
function ffn_check_if_changes
function ffn_check_required_fields
```

```
function ffn_save_data
sub fsb_clear
```

Save this project as something like TEMPLATE.MAK in the common global area in its own subdirectory. Make all the files associated with this project attribute read-only in DOS so you don't accidentally change anything later on.

Example:

```
\GLOBALS\TEMPLATE\ {contains}

            TEMPLATE.MAK

            TEMPLATE.FRM
```

Then, when you need to begin a new project, instead of starting from scratch, load this TEMPLATE.MAK. Remove any unnecessary VBXs and global BAS files from the project. Add any special files necessary for this particular application. Most of the files needed should already be included in TEMPLATE.MAK. Any of the calls or form-level shell routines on the form that are unnecessary to this particular program can be removed.

Pull up the template form and delete the objects that aren't required in this project. Duplicate necessary objects by clicking on them, pressing **Ctrl-Ins** to copy, then **Shift-Ins** to paste; say **No** to the VB question about creating a control array. Continue until the form has all the needed controls. Now **Save As** the Form and Project with the new application name in an appropriate directory. Using this method you guarantee all your applications will have the same default values. All forms will have the same color, border, and so forth. All controls will be the same size and font. Standard command buttons will be in the same order across the screen.

By using this template form approach you can save yourself a lot of time when starting a project. Setting each form and each control individually to a standard is tedious and prone to error. Guarantee consistency by using the template. It is more efficient than just a written standard that probably nobody will remember to read.

If your applications have several standard form types, then include one of each in the TEMPLATE.MAK. You might have a separate template for standard forms, popup forms, MDI parent and child

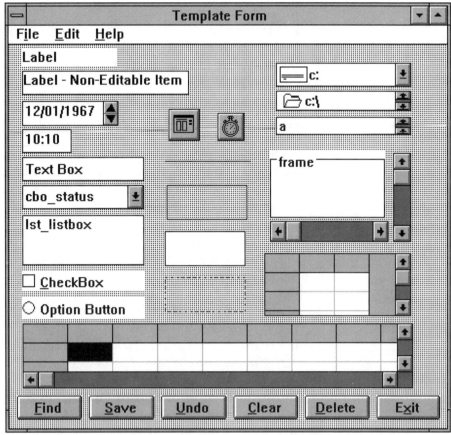

FIGURE 3.1 Sample template form.

forms, and so on. In each case, the template will save time and ensure consistency. This is also the easiest way to introduce a new programmer to your GUI standards and working environment. My template form looks something like Figure 3.1.

Psychedelic Forms

One technique that I think should never be used, but which I have had the misfortune of seeing in an application, is color-coding forms. The deranged developer decided to use a different background color for forms depending on their function. He used background colors of green, red, purple, and others, depending on whether the form was used for editing old data, add new data, reports, or whatever. It was a garish, horrible looking application. Whether it worked well didn't matter. The feeling users got was that they were in some creepy fun house at the carnival.

There are probably only three or four eye-pleasing Windows background colors to begin with. Even the good ones don't look good together. Do everyone's eyes a favor. Pick a standard background color for *all* applications and stick with it. Remember someone may be staring at the background color you select for eight hours a day. The best thing to do is take your sample template form and show it to someone in the Graphics department for comments.

Remember that your application's background colors won't necessarily display if not explicitly set at design time. A user can set a Windows default color scheme different from your own. Then all the forms and controls that you let default to your own color set will slide on over to HotDog or RotGut or whatever horrible setting they have. Those forms and controls you did explicitly set will not change. Now the application will really look like puke (Figure 3.2). Controls on the same form will be different colors.

I found this out because I use LCD Default Screen Settings as my Windows color scheme. I must set the background of text boxes and such to get them into our standard application color set. Other developers with a standard color set tend to let the controls default. On my PC, their programs usually come up in a grim latticework of alternating colors: half the controls are gray and the other half are white. Better than red and purple, but still not the way it's suppose to look. Explicitly set the colors on the template form and its controls, use it, and you won't have this problem.

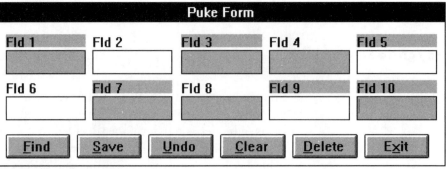

FIGURE 3.2 Puke form.

Font Wars

When my group first began applications development, there was a rather lengthy debate about both the type and size of the default screen font. If your group is having such a debate, then congratulations. The default font is as good a place as any to begin defining application standards. Don't think it's going to be easy. Yes, size does matter. Developers would love to set everything to a 2 point font so they can jam as much stuff on one form as possible. Small fonts seem kind of cool somehow. Small and dark and menacing. Big fonts look childish. We don't want no big Dumbo font. Of course, *we* won't be forced to use the application on a daily basis. The users supposedly need to be able to read the information that's on the screen.

The lofty academic debate is over whether to use a serif or sans serif font. I originally thought Sans Serif was the guy who designed the font in the first place. Actually, a serif is one of the fine cross lines at the edges of a letter. Sans serif fonts have no such lines. It is argued that a serif font is easier to read since these cross lines make each letter more distinctive. The original version of this book was in Helvetica and my brother refused to read it until I changed it to something serifishy like Times New Roman.

Compare and contrast:
Janson (serif):
The Quick Brown Fox Jumps Over The Lazy Dog.
Gill Sans (sans serif):
The Quick Brown Fox Jumps Over The Lazy Dog.

The argument is probably true with printed documents, but serif fonts on screen can be harder to read because the stray serif pixels can just make the letters more jagged. Sans or serif, you should limit your search only to the standard Windows fonts that will be available on everyone's PC. You might love that new *Ragamuffin-LumpenProle* font you ordered for $39.95 in the back of *Font Week* but remember, unless you install it on everyone's computer, that's not what they'll see. They'll all default to something else, maybe even regress back to Courier or LinePrinter. Geesh, your poor users will be living like Neanderthals.

The path of least resistance is to use the System font at the 9.75 point size. This is the Windows default font. Any complaints are answered with, "Hey, it's Windows default." OF COURSE NO MATTER WHICH FONT YOU DECIDE ON, DON'T USE ALL CAPITAL LETTERS FOR YOUR FORM HEADINGS, LABELS, AND MESSAGE BOXES. The effect is quite disturbing. I once saw an entire book written in all capital letters. I saw it. I couldn't bring myself to read it. Save all caps for grave warning messages about system failures or Martian invasions.

Screen Navigation : Just Wandering around Poking at Stuff

Although new users tend to use the mouse for navigation and special processing, experienced users rely on the keyboard to move around. Therefore, check the tab order of the controls on your form. Make sure someone moving through the form with the Tab key doesn't jump all over the place. Choose a standard tab flow for all forms, probably left to right, top to bottom, and stick to it.

The goal is 100 percent keyboard compliance for all operations performed on the form. I originally thought this was a stupid idea. Doesn't everyone running Windows have a mouse? While only the cruelest of companies would doom their employees to mouselessness, relying on it for simple operations quickly becomes annoying. The mouse seemed a lot cooler when you first started out in

Windows. The keyboard shortcuts, once they are known, are faster and more efficient.

Adding access keys to your form helps out in the keyboard compliance cause. An access key is created in a control's **Caption** property by putting an ampersand (&) in front of the letter you want to use. A menu item with a caption &File can then be accessed from the keyboard by typing **Alt-F**. Access keys are added to command buttons in the same manner. Remember not to use the same access key for two controls unless you've run out of unused letters.

Access keys can also be attached to controls that don't have a **Caption** property. You need to add a label next to the control and set an & in front of the appropriate letter in this label's caption. Set the label to a **TabIndex** one less than the control. When this label's access key is pressed, focus will shift to this other control since it's next in the tab order.

Test out each application by trying to do all the processing without using the mouse. If necessary, trap the **KeyPress** event on some controls to allow a mouse click to be duplicated on the keyboard. I'm thinking specifically of something like trapping the **Spacebar** press in a grid and calling the **Click** or **DblClick** event. The code would look something like this:

```
Sub grd_main_keypress(KeyAscii As Integer)
    If KeyAscii = KEY_SPACE Then
        Call grd_main_click
    End If
End Sub
```

One issue that can be a surprising sore spot with some users is that it's the **Tab** key, not the **Enter** key, that sets focus to the next field. This is especially true for data entry applications where users have come to expect the **Enter** key from years of DOS programs. It should be part of the basic Windows training you provide to actually show users how to move between fields. There is nothing sadder than watching a user lumber through a form wheeling the mouse to and fro then clicking on each field as if he or she were driving a stick shift.

The following transcript is taken from my own experience:
*"Umm, you know you can use the **Tab** key to move around," I explain.*

"Tab key? Whatszat? I press Enter and nothing hap-
pens." (The Enter key is then slammed six times as I'm
shot a haughty look, commonly know as the End-User
Glare) "I hate this system. It's junk. My hand is numb
from using the mouse."
"Try Tab," I plead. The user hopelessly scan all 101 keys,
perhaps for the first time in life. I lean over, point to the
key, then press it. The cursor springs to life, jumping
gamely to the next field in the tab order. The user stares
at the screen in disbelief.
"Yeah, but when I press Enter nothing happens."

You can solve this problem with help from the **KeyPress** event.
Let's look at how this could be done. Either perform the processing
at the field level: (used if only some fields process the **Enter** key).

For each field add the following code to the **KeyPress** event:

```
If KeyAscii = KEY_RETURN Then

    SendKeys "{Tab}"        'Press Tab Key

    KeyAscii = 0     'Remove Annoying Beep

End If
```

Or :

At the form level (everybody tabs at the **Enter** key): Set the Form's
Property **KeyPreview = True** to trap all keypresses before field-
level processing. Move the previous lines of code to the form-level
KeyPress event.

The problems with this scheme are:

★ It's tedious and it's overhead. You can easily forget an
instance if you do this processing at the field level. Your
diehard Enter pressers will then be marooned when they
get to this field. They'll hit **Enter**, won't look up, and keep
on typing. If it's a long text field, eventually they'll put all
the information on the form in it.

★ If you decide to do this only in a few special case applications, users must remember when they're in the Land of
Enter (read the transcript again). As always, consistency is
best.

★ Pressing the **Enter** key executes a command button. Users
will either end up executing every button that they try to

move off, or you'll have to tell them they need to use the **Tab** key in this special case. Ugh.

☆ Pressing the **Enter** key brings you to the next line in a text box if the property **MultiLine = True**. Users will either end up being thrown out of this field prematurely when they hit **Enter** to move to the next line, or you'll have to tell them they need to use the **Tab** key in this other special case. Ugh. Ugh.

☆ Who knows what **Enter** might be designed to process in a third-party VBX? Ugh. Ugh. Ugh.

I suggest that you try to get your users all aboard the Tab train. However, if you decide you really need to do this **Enter** thing then remember that users will also expect to use **Shift-Enter** to move back to the previous field. Oh sure, all those other fancy manuals tell you all about tabbing forward, but believe me, you better remember to include a **Shift-Enter** as well (read the transcript once more). If users can't remember to use the **Tab** key, they sure won't figure it out in reverse either. You can't trap **Shift-Enter** in the **KeyPress** event. You need to use **KeyDown**.

However, we have a delicate problem. If you put code in the **KeyPress** event to process the **Enter** key, this code will also get triggered by pressing **Shift-Enter**. If you are on **txt_two** and press **Shift-Enter**, your **KeyDown** event code will trigger first, setting focus to **txt_one**. Then the **KeyPress** event code will trigger setting focus back to **txt_two** and you don't go anywhere. We must remove the code we have in the **KeyPress** event and incorporate it into **KeyDown** or the cursor just sits there like a grump. This sort of extra event-triggering nonsense is covered again in the section in Chapter 5 "LostFocus/GetFocus : Get Like You Was before You Got Like You Is."

I wrote two global routines to perform this on a generic basic since this is what you are going to have to do if you go this route. Writing new code for each form would take an enormous amount of time. These are the global routines I wrote: **Sub gsb_Form_KeyDown** and **Function gfn_control_ok** (because **gsb_Form_KeyDown** is rather unwieldy and needed to be broken up).

```
Sub gsb_Form_KeyDown (ai_KeyCode As Integer, ai_Shift As Integer,
   ⇨a_frm As Form)

'Global routine to process Enter and Shift-Enter
```

```
Dim li_ctl As Integer
Dim li_taborder As Integer
Dim li_inc As Integer

Dim l_ctl_first As Control
Dim l_ctl_last As Control

If (ai_KeyCode = KEY_RETURN) Then

    'Get First And Last Control In TabOrder
    Set l_ctl_first = a_frm.ActiveControl
    Set l_ctl_last = a_frm.ActiveControl
    For li_ctl = 0 To a_frm.Controls.Count - 1 'Sweep Through All Controls
        If gfn_control_ok(a_frm.Controls(li_ctl)) = True Then
            If a_frm.Controls(li_ctl).TabIndex < l_ctl_first.TabIndex Then
                Set l_ctl_first = a_frm.Controls(li_ctl)
            ElseIf a_frm.Controls(li_ctl).TabIndex > l_ctl_last.TabIndex Then
                Set l_ctl_last = a_frm.Controls(li_ctl)
            End If
        End If
    Next li_ctl

    If ai_Shift = 1 Then 'ai_Shift-Return
        li_inc = -1
        If a_frm.ActiveControl.TabIndex = l_ctl_first.TabIndex Then
            l_ctl_last.SetFocus
            Exit Sub
        End If
    Else
        li_inc = 1
        If a_frm.ActiveControl.TabIndex = l_ctl_last.TabIndex Then
            l_ctl_first.SetFocus
            Exit Sub
        End If
    End If   'ai_Shift = 1

    li_taborder = li_inc

    Do While True
```

```
            For li_ctl = 0 To a_frm.Controls.Count - 1 'Sweep Through All
              ⇨Controls On Form
                If gfn_control_ok(a_frm.Controls(li_ctl)) = True Then
                  If a_frm.Controls(li_ctl).TabIndex =
                    ⇨(a_frm.ActiveControl.TabIndex + li_taborder) Then
                        a_frm.Controls(li_ctl).SetFocus
                        Exit Sub
                        End If
                End If
            Next li_ctl

            li_taborder = li_taborder + li_inc

       Loop

   End If    '(ai_KeyCode = KEY_RETURN)

   End Sub

Function gfn_control_ok (a_ctl As Control) As Integer
     'Function determines if you can tab onto the control
     'Called from sub gsb_Form_KeyDown

     gfn_control_ok = False
     'This is a list of controls that can't get focus so must be ignored
     If TypeOf a_ctl Is CommonDialog Then            'ignore
     ElseIf TypeOf a_ctl Is Data Then                'ignore
     ElseIf TypeOf a_ctl Is Frame Then               'ignore
     ElseIf TypeOf a_ctl Is Image Then               'ignore
     ElseIf TypeOf a_ctl Is Label Then               'ignore
     ElseIf TypeOf a_ctl Is Line Then                'ignore
     ElseIf TypeOf a_ctl Is Menu Then                'ignore
     ElseIf TypeOf a_ctl Is OLEClient Then           'ignore
     ElseIf TypeOf a_ctl Is Shape Then               'ignore
     ElseIf TypeOf a_ctl Is Timer Then               'ignore
     'Tab only to an enabled control with a TabStop = True and Visible = True
     ElseIf (a_ctl.Enabled = True) And (a_ctl.TabStop = True) And
         ⇨(a_ctl.Visible = True) Then
       gfn_control_ok = True
     End If
End Function
```

Calling procedure in **Form_KeyDown** event:

```
Sub Form_KeyDown (KeyCode As Integer, Shift As Integer)

    Call gsb_Form_KeyDown (KeyCode, Shift, Me)

End Sub
```

Also include the following line in the form **KeyPress** event to remove the annoying beep:

```
Sub Form_KeyPress (KeyAscii As Integer)

    If KeyAscii = KEY_RETURN Then

        KeyAscii = 0 'Stop the beep

    End If

End Sub
```

Remember, you also need to set **KeyPreview = True** on all forms that call this routine.

Why is there so much code to do this? Whenever you go against the grain in Windows, you get your skin ripped off. We must avoid setting focus in the following situations:

1. Can't set focus to a field that has **Enabled = False** (hard crash).
2. Can't set focus to a field that has **Visible = False** (hard crash).
3. Can't set focus to these control types: CommonDialog, Data, Frame, Image, Label, Line, Menu, OleClient, Shape, Timer (hard crash).
4. Shouldn't tab to a field with **TabStop = False** (if set to False then it's not in the tab order).
5. Need to set focus back to the first field when tabbing off last field (consistency with normal tab processing).
6. Need to set focus back to the last field when back tabbing off first field (consistency with normal tab processing).

Is it ugly? Oh yeah. I'm not going to lie to you like the code example on page 424 of the *Visual Basic 3.0 Programmer's Guide*. It's the same **Enter** processing jizz, but what about all the special cases? Just too messy to deal with I guess. I was growling like a bear when I wrote this example. I'm sure not going to use it (the **Tab** key's good enough for me), but you deserve to know the whole truth.

Now, I'm not suggesting you use this code or even consider doing such processing. Don't. Forget about it. Just realize what you can get yourself up against when your development group decides they want to "kernel hack" and make Windows do things it doesn't want to do. We're trying to get a four-year-old to eat brussel sprouts here. Remember "Odd Oaths in Design Review?" Rewriting all your applications to process the **Enter** key would fit in rather nicely with the rest of the sordid lot.

However, purely as a sipping-amarettos-in-a-pancled-den academic exercise, you can see we got to use a lot of the tricks mentioned in "Global Routines: The Lazy Man's Friend" in Chapter 2:

☆ Argument prefixing.

☆ ActiveControl.

☆ Passing a form and a control as argument variables.

☆ If TypeOf *object* Is *objecttype* logic.

☆ Using the controls collection to sweep through all the controls on the form.

This code example will work for the standard default VB control set. If you have additional controls that you can't set focus to, then you need to add them to function gfn_control_ok as additional **ElseIf TypeOf a_ctl Is *control* Then** parameters. Likewise, if you haven't included all the standard controls in your project, you must comment out the lines that refer to these controls in **gfn_control_ok**. Otherwise you'll suffer the inevitable "Type not defined" error.

Are you wondering why nobody mentioned **Shift-Enter**? There's probably an API call that would make this process easier, but as you can see, I don't know it. I haven't explored this topic any further because I've avoided the whole mess by using good old **Tab**.

Menus: Right Wing Fringe

When designed improperly, menus have the power to stun and disorient. The first step in alleviating menu confusion is establishing your typical menu layout on the template form. Without this base, your applications will end up with standard menu options in different locations. Such inconsistencies greatly annoy users. Standard menu option locations and keyboard equivalents should be as consistent as possible. Any new menu items added to the program should include access key and function key equivalents where appropriate. The reason for special care in menu design is, quite honestly, that menus intimidate many users. Menus are stark, wordy lists that jump out at them. There are underscores, check marks, and ellipses (...). **Shift-Alt-F12**, **Ctrl-Alt-F5**, and **Shift-F1** attack from the right side. Some options are gray but users don't know why.

Remember, the longer the number of items on the menu, the more intimidated the user. Determine if a separate main menu item can be created to hold some of the items on the list. Break up your list with separator bars to group like processes together. It's best to keep these sections to about five items. I once created a menu that went clear down to the end of the screen, and the users went nuts. I put the items into several smaller menus and added separator bars. Some options I removed altogether and placed on a button bar. Everyone still hates it, but it's far less confusing.

Also be careful of making the menus too many levels deep. A menu with two nested levels is tricky for users. Any more and you create a crooked menu staircase gracelessly drifting to the right of the screen (Figure 3.3). Users don't know how to back out of these contraptions and end up executing a selection accidentally.

One thing I've discovered is that if an operation is found only on the menu, new users won't find it. New users don't even consider looking for anything on the menu. They just stare helplessly at the screen. I was also amazed at what an awful burden I placed on users by requiring them to select items from a menu. "I have to click it and then highlight the selection," they moan. "I don't want to have to do that. Everything should just happen automatically."

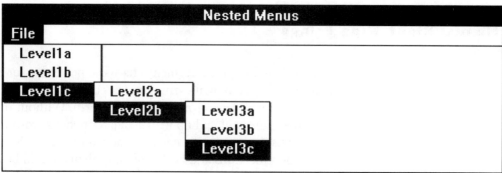

FIGURE 3.3 Help, I'm Stuck!

```
┌─────────────────────────────────────────────────────────────┐
│ ─     MDI Parent With Button Bar                        ▼  ▲ │
├───────┬────────┬────────┬────────┬─────────┬────────────────┤
│ Find  │ Save   │ Undo   │ Clear  │ Delete  │ Exit           │
├───────┴────────┴────────┴────────┴─────────┴────────────────┤
│                                                             │
│                                                             │
│                                                             │
└─────────────────────────────────────────────────────────────┘
```

FIGURE 3.4 MDI form with button bar.

My experience has shown that users prefer buttons, a screen-wide expanse of buttons with words on them. I don't mean those graphics-only buttons with nothing but a weird symbol on their bellies either—you know the ones, a firing squad on the Execute button, windshield wipers on the Clear button. Put one of those on your form, and they'll keep asking what it means. You'll really feel like a jerk having to explain your cute little picture as they look at you like you're some dysfunctional child. Save the pictures for the icons.

In MDI applications you can create a button bar on the MDI Parent (Figure 3.4). MDI Parent forms don't like to have controls put on them. They give some weird message about align properties, as if anyone actually read the manual and knows what that means. You first need to put a picture box on the form. Then you can left-click the mouse on desired control in the VB toolbox, move to the picture box on the MDI form, left-click and drag the mouse, thus sneaking the control onto the form. You can smuggle any desired controls onto the MDI form in this manner.

One last tidbit. Putting **Char(8)** before the last main menu item places it in the right corner of the form (Figure 3.5). This is useful

```
┌─────────────────────────────────────────────────────────────┐
│                      Right Wing Fringe                       │
├─────────────────────────────────────────────────────────────┤
│ File   Reports                                         Help  │
│                                                             │
│                                                             │
│                                                             │
│                                                             │
│                                                             │
└─────────────────────────────────────────────────────────────┘
```

FIGURE 3.5 Right-justified Help menu item.

for something like the Help menu option.

```
mnu_help.Caption = Chr(8) + mnu_help.Caption
```

Communicating with the User: Beep That I May See Thee

Whatcha Doing?

Before any lengthy processing, set the **MousePointer = HOUR-GLASS**. I'd say anything over five seconds is a lengthy process. If you don't put up the hourglass during an extended wait, users get an itchy trigger finger and start clicking madly at the screen. All these clicks pile up in the queue. When your processing is finished, the ricochets can be deadly. Be sure to set **MousePointer = DEFAULT** when the process is finished. Forgetting to remove the hourglass is worse than not using it at all. A permanent hourglass pointer is the universal sign to reboot the machine.

If you're churning through a big process like importing records and you can accurately measure your progress, consider putting up a status bar or gauge showing the percentage of processing completed. For some reason, people will endure an agonizing wait if they have

FIGURE 3.6 Better Than Just A Beep.

some idea how far along they are. This is why amusement parks post signs along the line to a ride saying, "One Hour Wait from This Point." But if you make your users wait an hour, you better put up a little more than a sign. Dancing bears, perhaps?

Beep, Beep

In general, users hate beeps: (I've overhead the following user/computer dialog)

Beep.
"Why does it keep beeping at me?"
Beep.
"It keeps beeping at me!"
Beep.
"Stop it!!! @#$%!&!!!"

That's a very telling exchange. The key word isn't *beep*, it's *why*. A beep doesn't really communicate that much information. To the user, the rough translation is "You Idiot!" Your program should communicate as clearly as possible what it wants from the user. Generally, it's better to put up a message box telling users what they are doing wrong instead of giving them the old "Beep You" (Figure 3.6). In this case, the user presses the Add button without selecting an item from the list box and is then tutored with a message box, not vexed by a beep.

The Deep Structure of Message Boxes

We have explored using a global BAS file for standard messages. Working through your standard processing application will help you decide what standard message boxes you'll need to include in this file. My only further suggestion is to decide on the actual sentence structure for all messages displayed in your applications. This may seem insignificant but at least consider it. The following messages tell the same story but with a slight twist.

"The processing is complete."
"The Processing Is Complete"
"The Processing Is Complete."
"Processing Complete"
"Processing complete"
"Processing complete."
"processing complete"

You get the point. Decide on typical statement syntax and whether to use full sentences, short phrases, initial caps, periods, and so on.

This requires just a small amount of effort but adds to the illusion that the application is tight and consistent.

GUI Design: The Big Lie

Windows magazines and journals writers have fallen in love with calling objects and controls screen metaphors, although I doubt any of them will end up in poetry anytime soon: "Your eyes are check boxes; your lips, two drop-down combos . . . ." I prefer to call them lies. Smiling faces hiding the awful truth. No, dear user, your data isn't stored as a cute little check mark, it's saved as -1. You know that combo item you selected that said "Happy Bunny?" We get its unique ID value and save it as 31997. See that shiny animated command button with the puppy dog jumping out of the box? You know, the one you press to save the data. When it gets clicked, about a thousand lines of twisted, agonizing code get executed. If the application keeps up its poker face long enough, the user is convinced of the biggest lie of all, "My how simple this all is. So serene. I can't understand why it took 18 months to develop." The way we pull off this big lie is through good screen design. We must create the facade that everything is going along just swimmingly, because if users could actually see what's behind all those buttons and gizmos, they'd never use a computer again. The previous chapters have given us a good base for our cozy little lie. Let's just look at a few control-level details we also need to remember.

Always Tell the Same Lie: Consistent Screen Metaphors

If an application has several forms that must represent the values Y or N for the field ISACTIVE, we have several choices (Figure 3.7):

Check box:	Caption = Active When it's checked, the value saved is Y; unchecked the value saved is N.
Drop-down combo box:	Contains two items: Active and Inactive Active is saved as Y; Inactive is saved as N.
Option buttons:	One button is titled Active, the other Inactive. Again, Active is saved as Y; Inactive is saved as N.
Text box:	Input character is limited to only Y or N.

None of these is necessarily worse than the others. It's nice to have all these choices, but the last thing you want is four forms each representing the same data element a different way. If we end up telling the users a different story on each form, they won't believe any of them. I think this problem is most common to new developers who can't wait to try out all the controls that beckon from the toolbox. Your application is not a video game. The users aren't looking for a new challenge every time a form is displayed.

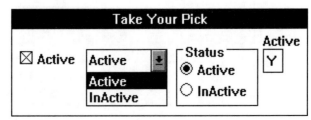

FIGURE 3.7 Take Your Pick

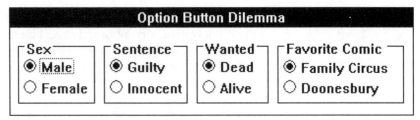

FIGURE 3.8 Option button dilemma.

Sex and the Drop-Down Combo: Use an Appropriate Control for the Data Item

Some screen lies are harder to believe than others. Don't use two option buttons for the representation of a male/female field. By defaulting to either male or female, it looks like you're taking sides. Use the combo box with Style-2: Dropdown List. Consider this each time you decide to use an option button.

I recently bought a Personality Assessment program. It used an option button to represent male/female (Figure 3.8). Neither option button was the default, but the program didn't require one to be selected. Instead, it defaulted to female when generating the assessment. I failed to notice this until after I read my report and discovered I enjoy wearing high heels and silky lingerie. Some print jobs are best not sent to the warehouse laserjet.

Command Buttons: My What Big Eyes You Have

When you make really big command buttons (actually the VB default size is a little too big) the effect is cartoonish (Figure 3.9).

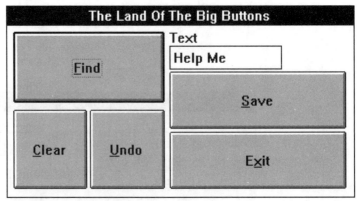

FIGURE 3.9 The land of the big buttons.

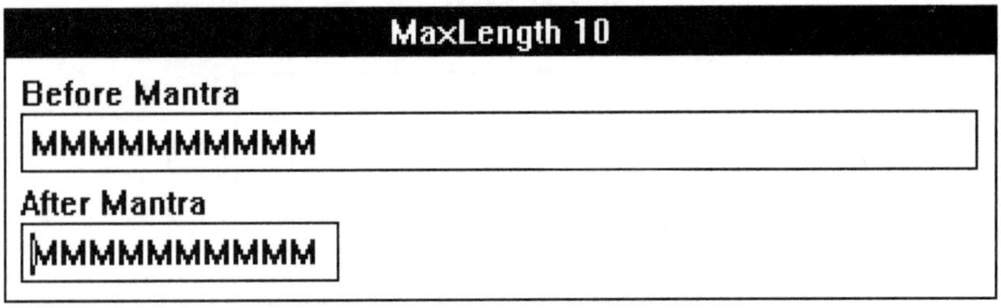

FIGURE 3.10 MaxLength 10.

Keep them small, and make all the buttons on the form the same size. Buttons are like the form's eyes. If their size varies wildly, the effect is creepy.

Text Boxes: Mmm, Good

Text boxes have a **MaxLength** property. If you leave the property at the default of 0, you can put a whole lot of text in that box. You don't want users pouring out their hearts and souls in a comment text box that gets saved as a trim 10-character field. Each text box **MaxLength** property should be set to the field's size in the database. This is a very easy and very important thing to do. Don't risk trimming real data. The good stuff is always at the end.

After the **MaxLength** property is set, the text box should be sized appropriately. Don't make a text box any bigger than it has to be. Users will wonder why they can't go on anymore when there's still all that empty space just up ahead. Use the old M technique. If the **MaxLength** is 10, set the **Text** property to **MMMMMMMMMM**, then resize the control (Figure 3.10). Remove this mantra when you're finished.

List Boxes: On the Count of Ten

Most programs are good about setting the property **Sorted = True** for list boxes and combo boxes. If you have a list box with the property **Sorted = True**, then don't spoil the party by specifying an index when you issue an **AddItem** command. That item goes just where you tell it to, and that's the end of your sort.

The other problem with using the **Sorted** property is with numeric values. If you load numeric values in the list box you'll end up with a sort order like in Figure 3.11. That's not how I count, but the list box doesn't know any better. You'll need to do this with an unsorted list box and indexed add items. If this process doesn't scream out

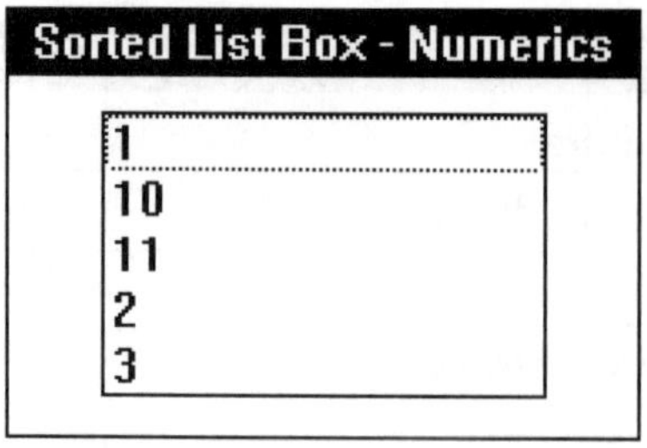

FIGURE 3.11 Sorted list box — numerics.

"Global Routine," I don't know what does. You can try a sorted list box with numerics if you use the **Format** command. First determine the maximum number of digits before and after the decimal point. Let's say three before and two after. Now add an item like this:

```
lst_numeric.AddItem Format(Str(li_value), "000.00")
```

The results are shown in Figure 3.12. Too ugly? Maybe. This technique will also only work if the numerics are positive. Negatives ruin the whole thing. Well, I tried.

Straight and on the Level

A Windows form is not the place for hip, deconstructed design. Don't lose points for sloppiness. If your controls stagger around the form, you'll give users vertigo (Figure 3.13). A horizontal row of controls should all line up (Figure 3.14). A vertical display should plum straight down. Select all the controls in the group and set the Top or Left property all the same. Think of the form as a grid, not as crazed, naked abandonment. Aligning controls is the simple and obvious thing to do, so if you forget, users will really lambaste you.

Screen lies. Doesn't that make more sense? Metaphors. Please.

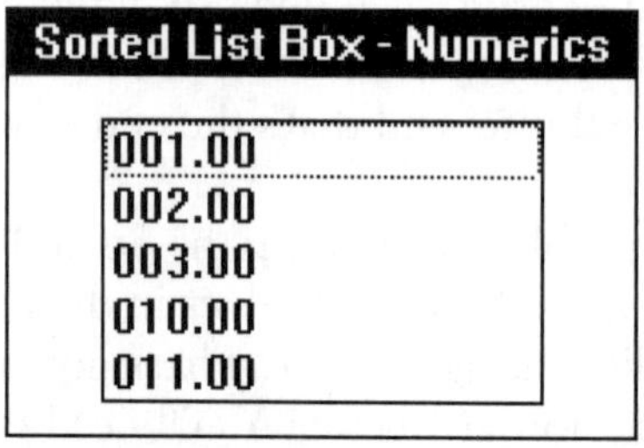

FIGURE 3.12 Sorted list box — numerics (instead).

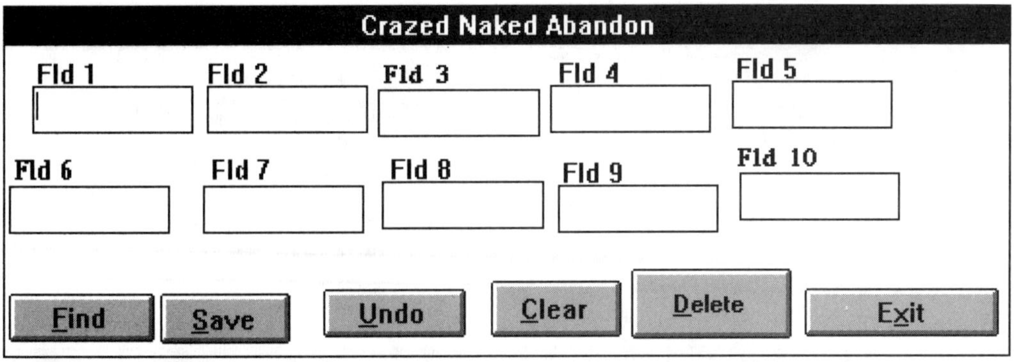

FIGURE 3.13 Drunken form.

Lost but Not Forgotten : Deleting Objects from a Form

If you have code behind an object on a form and you delete this object, your code remains behind, a ghostly reminder of programming past. To see this orphaned code, bring up the form's code window. Select (**general**) from the Object box and then look in the Procedure list box.

Remember, if you rename an object after you put code behind it, all the code gets lost and wanders into the (**general**) area (Figure 3.15). To get the code back, set the control's **Name** property to its original value. To prevent this problem, always set the appropriate name for your objects before writing any code behind them.

This weirdness can work to your advantage in certain situations. (The following example is cool but tricky. Test drive before buying.) Say you have an existing group of code-filled control(s) that now need to go into a frame as a result of a screen redesign. You can

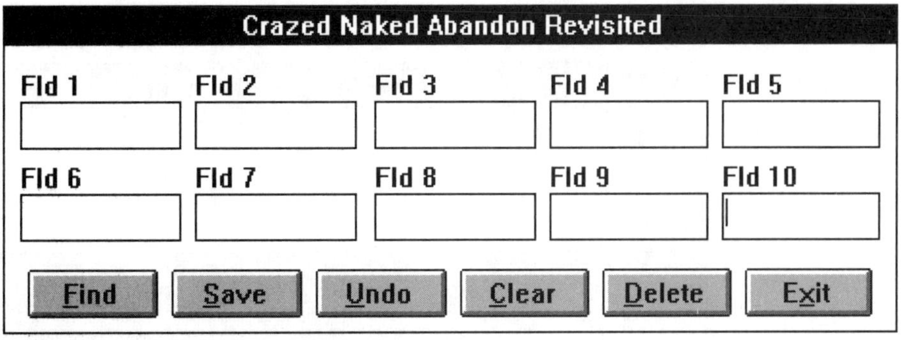

FIGURE 3.14 Sobered up form.

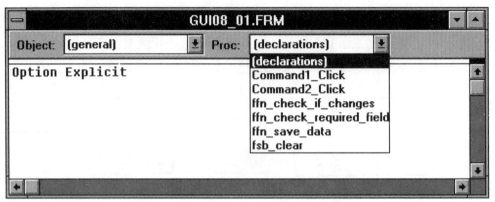

FIGURE 3.15 Command1 and Command2 are orphaned procedures.

select the group, then copy it to the Clipboard with **Ctrl-Ins** (Figure 3.16). Now delete the group of controls (Figure 3.17). Select the frame and do **Shift-Ins** to paste the group of controls into it (Figure 3.18). Now the controls will move as a group with the frame. You'll see all your old code is still there. Practice, please.

Windows Training: One Click Makes You Smaller

After you've worked in Windows a while, you can really tear around. You load separate programs, then minimize them on the workspace. After that, you switch back and forth, cutting and pasting between them. There are lots of cool icons and gizmos to delight the eye and spirit. What you forget is that although it seems really simple and intuitive, Windows is not easy to learn. Users migrating from the gentle DOS fields of one app at a time have a bit of culture shock when they get thrown into the busy Windows environment. Users presented with this overload get frustrated and annoyed.

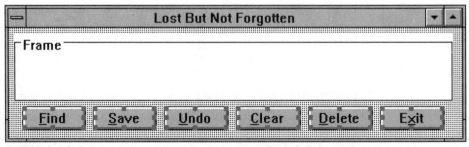

FIGURE 3.16 Select all the control buttons, then **Ctrl_Ins** to copy.

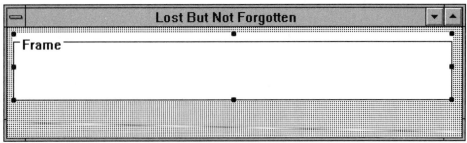

FIGURE 3.17 Select all the control buttons again, then press Delete to remove the Controls, select the frame, then **Shift-Ins** to paste.

Now, if you're one of the new home computer enthusiasts, you probably think this is ridiculous. Your computer probably came pre-loaded with Windows, and maybe you've never even seen a DOS prompt. Well my dear homebody, there are thousands of old computers still used in companies today that you would've expected to find in a relics museum next to the UNIVAC. There are monochrome monitors of orange or green, 10 meg hard drives and upgraded XTs. Many people just go into e-mail and that's about it. The need to use your application may finally upgrade a user's computer. Behold, a shiny 486 and Windows in all its splendor. Now what do I do?

The general feeling is that Windows is intuitive, and any new user will jump in and find the water's just fine. As a result, little or no training is given. The user may then thrash around for months, intimidated and overwhelmed. This tormented user can be anybody: a renowned Ph.D. or big-shot executive can flounder as hopelessly as anyone else (actually they tend to flounder more). A cruel developer might say, "Good, let 'em suffer. It's been agony developing this system. It should be agony to use it." Besides being hard-hearted, that's a rather short-sighted view, since unhappy users

FIGURE 3.18 The command buttons have moved into the frame yet maintain all attached code.

do not suffer in silence. Believe me, you want happy, well-fed users for your own sake.

Users unfamiliar with standard Windows operation, controls, and appearance may be overwhelmed even before they log in to your application. They need to practice, hands on, with something soft, simple, and nonthreatening. A complicated in-house application running live with critical data does not meet any of those criteria. I suggest you offer some form of basic Windows training to all users. If you don't have the staff (we don't), then buy a Windows how-to videotape and a beginner's book. You can tell it's a beginner's book because it usually has the word stupid, idiot, moron, or half-wit in the title. This seems a bit insulting to me, but it's all the rage.

Any training session, whether it is basic Windows stuff or application specific, should be hands-on if at all possible. No one learns anything sitting there watching you zoom around. They watch, nod in agreement, and don't remember a thing. I know that's what I do. Start out with bunny fur programs. Solitaire and Paintbrush are good. They aren't scary and give the mouse hand a good workout. Have everyone sit close together so they start talking and learn from each other. The best instructor to a new user is often someone who just figured it out themselves.

Remember, new users don't know the screen lies to which you have grown so accustomed. I suggest you make a small application, actually just a single form, that contains at least one of each object that might be included in one of your applications. Perhaps you can use a modified version of your template form for this (Figure 3.19). You can include the standard processing command buttons or menu items and even launch some of your global popup forms or VB's common dialog boxes. This gets users familiar with some of the features they'll be encountering in your real applications. Explain that the form does nothing, doesn't save data, and won't break no matter what they do to it. Let them just play around for a while, tabbing between controls and discovering what each object does. After some play time, briefly describe each object and standard processing. Keep any explanations simple and don't start talking about device drivers and memory managers. Keep in mind that there's usually more than one way to do just about everything in Windows. Don't think you're being helpful when you rattle them all off at once. Presented with several options, the user will forget all of them.

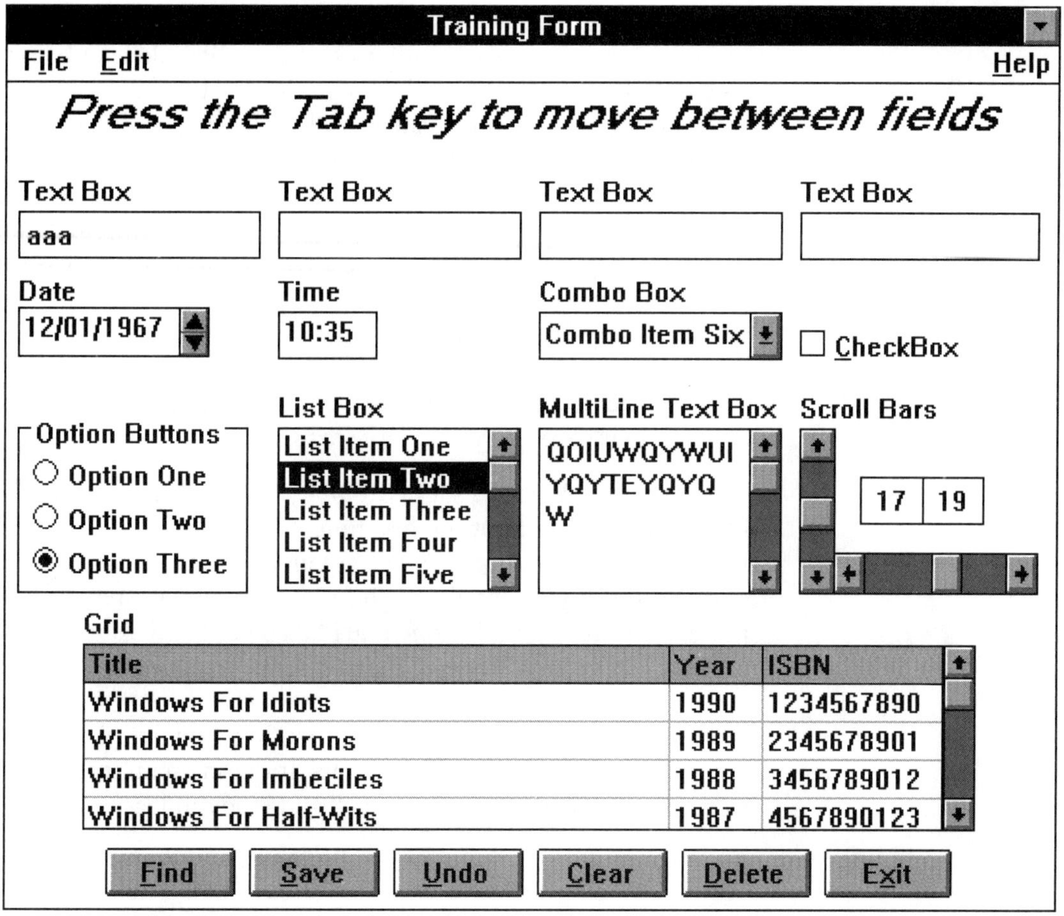

FIGURE 3.19 Modified template form used for training.

Here's the most common simple Windows problem I encountered during my tenure on the company's help desk. It's worth going over in a training class. Users load an application. They then inadvertently click on the Windows workspace and this application disappears. Where is it? They don't know. Sometimes they panic. Users can end up in the same bad state by accidentally minimizing the application. Either way, they load the program all over again. I've seen six copies of an application sitting minimized on a user's machine. Some applications won't run a second time; instead, they complain that multiple copies are loaded. Of course, the user has no idea what to do. Users need to know that the application didn't completely disappear and how they can find it again. Show them how to use **Alt-Tab** to cycle through current applications and how **Ctrl-Esc** brings up the Task List. Save yourself some help desk calls.

Empathize with anyone who is frustrated during a training session, and tell them you think Windows sucks too. People hate being told it's easy if they try. "I love Windows, it's easy. Even my hamster enjoys working with spreadsheets in Excel. You just don't make an effort to learn it. You better catch on or you're going end up as a roustabout at the carnival." That might work with a kid. Adults will turn to stone. There's a three-step process when trying to help people when they're having trouble. Convey the following ideas in the order listed below.

1. There is a problem.
2. It is not your fault.
3. The problem can be resolved. It won't be easy, but you can do it because you're very smart.

"You're right, Windows sucks. It's not you. It isn't in your head. Only nerds figure it out the first time. Twisted freaks, all of them. Filthy, dirty mutant dogs. You've got an advantage though. They don't have half your intellect. Those sick, awful monsters. If I can just explain this logically, someone like you can make some sense of it. Now let's go over some of the problems this thing is causing you."

Granted, I'm the only person in the world who talks like that but you get the point. Is the chatter true? It doesn't matter. Your goal is to get this person's confidence back and ready to learn.

X-Ray Eyes

Despite all your efforts, you can still end up with a screen design that will confuse and frustrate users. One reason is that programmers tend to view their programs with X-ray eyes, barely noticing the interface. We're concerned with what's going on under the hood. Even when viewing other applications, I'm looking clear through those brushed-steel 3-D controls wondering about the ugly truth inside. After writing acres of impossibly complicated code, you can't believe all anyone notices is that the text boxes are misaligned.

The best way to see if your design makes any sense is to show it to someone who has no idea what your program is supposed to do. This is actually the only way to seriously test the screen design. The entire development team eventually gets so used to the standard processing and interface that they take it for granted. You need a new set of eyes.

Sit the person down in front of the computer and launch the application. Insist right off that you are not looking for positive comments. Make it clear that it's the screen design being judged, not the reviewer. You don't want someone holding back comments because he or she is afraid to look stupid. Remember, once the real users get hold of the system, they'll show no mercy and feel no remorse.

Watch the reviewer's face as the form is displayed. Get an immediate reaction. Ask, "What draws your eye? What area of the screen looks confusing?" Explain the basic processing and let him or her try to do it without any further instruction. Most important, have the reviewer say out loud everything that's going through his or her mind. Keep asking, "What's not clear? What would you do to make it better?" Demand specifics. Write everything down. Don't sigh, don't grimace, don't throw up your hands. This person is telling the truth. You're going to learn more this way than I could write about in a thousand pages.

CHAPTER *four*

SQL

Intro to SQL: JAWS II

I've mentioned before that the main reason a corporate application exists is to process data. Nobody wants that program I always see as an example in programming books. It has a text box, a command button, and a label. You type in the temperature in degrees Fahrenheit, press the command button, and the temperature converted to Celsius appears in the label (Figure 4.1). If a program like this did exist, it would probably have to process several thousand temperatures stored in a database table. The program would display the records, possibly filtering them based on certain criteria. The users would probably be allowed to add, modify, and delete these records. On a regular basis, one or more standard reports on the data would have to be generated.

Temperature Convert

Farenheit

100

Celsius

37.8

Convert   Exit

FIGURE 4.1 You've got to be kidding.

Most likely, your applications will use some variation of SQL or Structured Query Language to perform these tasks. Performing this processing using standard flat-file I/O can be wicked and should be reserved for very simple applications. SQL is a lot more fun. SQL is pronounced "sequel" by everyone but me. I still say "S-Q-L" and everyone looks at me like I'm a potato farmer. It was created by IBM, which, to my knowledge, everyone pronounces the same way. SQL is amazingly powerful and easy to learn. As a programmer, you can perform all the data manipulation you need with four statements. I'll base my examples here on this mythical temperature program. There are two tables used: SAMPLES, which contains the temperature readings, and S_INFO, which contains specific information about the samples themselves.

The tables look like this:

```
SAMPLES Table

SAMPLE_ID Integer

TEMP_FAREN Float
```

Example data in table:

```
SAMPLE_ID   TEMP_FAREN

1           100

2           75

3           57


S_INFO Table

SAMPLE_ID      Integer

SAMPLE_NAME    Char(50)

COMMENTS       Char(100)
```

Example data in table:

```
SAMPLE_ID   SAMPLE_NAME   COMMENTS

1           Test Run 37   Pending

2           Sample B      Not sure

3           Lab Check     Done earlier
```

Here are the four SQL statements:
SELECT—retrieves a set of records.

```
SELECT

    SAMPLE_ID, TEMP_FAREN, (TEMP_FAREN - 32) * 5/9

FROM
```

```
        SAMPLES
WHERE
        TEMP_FAREN > 0
ORDER BY
        SAMPLE_ID
```

Returns:

```
SAMPLE_ID    TEMP_FAREN    (TEMP_FAREN - 32) * 5/9

1            100           37.7

2            75            23.8

3            57            13.8
```

(TEMP_FAREN - 32) * 5/9 is an example of a computed column that doesn't really exist in the table.

Fields from more than one table can be retrieved in a single SQL SELECT statement by joining the tables through common key field(s). Next, I retrieve the TEMP_FAREN field from the SAMPLES table and the SAMPLE_NAME field from the S_INFO table. The two tables are linked by the key field SAMPLE_ID, which exists in both tables.

```
SELECT
        S_INFO.SAMPLE_NAME, SAMPLES.TEMP_FAREN
FROM
        SAMPLES, S_INFO
WHERE
        SAMPLES.SAMPLE_ID = S_INFO.SAMPLE_ID
```

Retrieves:

```
SAMPLE_NAME      TEMP_FAREN

Test Run 37      100

Sample B         75

Lab Check        57
```

INSERT—adds a new record.

```
INSERT INTO SAMPLES
        (SAMPLE_ID, TEMP_FAREN)
VALUES
        (4, 54)
```

UPDATE—updates fields in one or more existing records.

```
UPDATE
      SAMPLES
SET
      TEMP_FAREN = 55
WHERE
      SAMPLE_ID = 1
```

DELETE—deletes one or more existing records.

```
DELETE FROM
      SAMPLES
WHERE
      SAMPLE_ID = 1
```

That's just a little taste. A good SQL manual will explain the basics better than I do. I will go over two basic SQL errors and several advanced techniques that I have actually needed to use, unlike the advanced techniques in the SQL manual that nobody would ever think to use. I am using standard or semi-standard SQL for my examples. You may be working with a weirder form of SQL but the concepts will be the same. Test out any of the statements I write to make sure they perform in your environment.

Basic SQL Errors: Too Much or Not Enough

Here's a simple SQL SELECT statement:

```
SELECT
      EMP_ID, F_NAME, L_NAME, M_INIT, STATUS_CD, COMMENTS
FROM
      EMPLOYEE
WHERE
      STATUS_CD = 1
ORDER BY
      L_NAME, F_NAME, M_INIT
```

It should be fairly obvious what this statement does. It retrieves the EMP_ID, F_NAME, L_NAME, M_INIT, STATUS_CD, COM-MENTS columns from the EMPLOYEE table for all records

where the STATUS_CD = 1. The retrieved records will be sorted
in ascending order by L_NAME, F_NAME, M_INIT. Simple SQL
SELECT statements (basically statements using only one table)
probably won't cause much trouble. But there is trouble. It comes
when more than one table is used in the SELECT statement.

The two most common SQL SELECT troubles are:

★ Not enough records.

★ Getting too many records, sometimes so many the statement takes forever to execute, and you wonder whether to
  reboot the machine.

Here's a statement where the first problem is brewing: It's the previous statement joined with the STATUS table.

```
STATUS

CODE  Integer

VALUE Char(20)
```

Example data in table:

```
CODE  VALUE

1     Active

2     Terminated

3     Maternity Leave

4     Disability Leave


SELECT

      EMP_ID, F_NAME, L_NAME, M_INIT, STATUS.VALUE, COMMENTS

FROM

      EMPLOYEE, STATUS

WHERE

      EMPLOYEE.STATUS_CD = STATUS.CODE
```

In this SQL statement, the EMPLOYEE and STATUS tables are
joined by the field STATUS_CD. The purpose of the join is to display the value associated with the STATUS_CD field instead of the
STATUS_CD itself that is just a number. This is a very common
SQL thing you need to do. Let's say there are 200 records in the
table and you're only getting 180 records back. What's the problem? This brings you to the most important questions you need
answered about a field involved in a join:

1. Are the fields being joined guaranteed to match each other?
2. If there isn't a match, should I retrieve the record anyway?

So let's ask these questions in this particulare case:

Does EMPLOYEE.STATUS_CD always match with a STATUS.CODE?

If it doesn't match, do I still want the EMPLOYEE record?

If STATUS_CD can be left blank in EMPLOYEE, then it won't match STATUS and won't return a record. In this case, I don't want that to happen so I must rewrite the statement slightly. When doing a join like this one, where the field joining the two tables can be blank (or just isn't guaranteed to match), you need an outer join. Here it is:

```
SELECT
        EMP_ID, F_NAME, L_NAME, M_INIT, STATUS.VALUE, COMMENTS
FROM
        EMPLOYEE, STATUS
WHERE
        EMPLOYEE.STATUS_CD *= STATUS.CODE
```

The *= says that all records should be retrieved from the table on the left side of the equal sign, here EMPLOYEE. If there is a match, then also retrieve the value from the table on the right side of the equal sign, here STATUS.

Not using an outer join when necessary is the most common cause of retrieving fewer records than expected. I've done it, and had to maintain several programs from other people that had this error. One was a personnel application that used a code/value for the RESPONSIBILITY field. The retrieve did a join but didn't require the RESPONSIBILITY field to be filled in. A user would add a bunch of personnel without entering a RESPONSIBILITY, save, then none of the records would display even though they were in the database.

I've also encountered this problem in programs that were originally set up to require the user to enter an appropriate value for the joining field. The SQL call started out working just fine. The specs for the program then changed, making the field optional, but the original SELECT statement didn't get changed. A very simple bug that can ruin your day. Check if any such situations occurred if you've inherited an old project.

The second problem happens less frequently but when it does, watch out. Here's a statement where trouble #2 is brewing:

```
SELECT
        EMP_ID, F_NAME, L_NAME, M_INIT, STATUS.VALUE, COMMENTS
FROM
        EMPLOYEE, STATUS, SALARY
WHERE
        EMPLOYEE.STATUS_CD *= STATUS.CODE
```

This statement returns a zillion records after a considerable delay. Why?

The problem is insidious because you'd think it wouldn't really be a problem. This statement has an extra table in its FROM clause that is not used in the WHERE clause. The result is SQL matches every record in this table with every record retrieved in a process called a Cartesian Product. This result isn't quite as elegant as it sounds; it's actually nothing more than a Big Mess. The number of records retrieved will vary considerably depending on the number of tables in the join and the number of records in the tables. If your tables have just a few records, you may not notice the extra records retrieved, but once those tables start to fill up, you'll be languishing in decadent excess.

The person who wrote this statement either:
1. Forgot to add the connection to it in the WHERE clause.
2. Shouldn't have included this extra table in the FROM clause.

Often, the second case occurs when someone is optimizing a large SQL statement. They realize, "Hey, I don't need this in the WHERE clause," and remove the join, forgetting that the table is still in the FROM clause. I know this happens because my boss did it. Three people looked at the statement for 20 minutes before the problem was discovered. Save your people and your minutes; look for it first. The best thing to do is to print out the SQL, then go over it making sure all tables in the FROM clause are actually being used.

If you use a SELECT DISTINCT statement, the second error will hide from you. SQL still retrieves the zillion records into its own temporary table but will then filter out the endless duplicates, displaying just the unique records to you. The poor server must chug away, a helpless accessory to your destructive plan. The DISTINCT clause is very useful in certain situations. Just make sure it isn't covering up some erroneous and terribly inefficient SQL. Do a zillion record retrieve check of the SQL statement without the DISTINCT clause, then put it in.

Hysterical Warning:

If you want to try out an example of error #2 just to see it in action then make sure you use tables that have about two records in them and include only one unnecessary table in the join. This can really be a killer statement. Please don't torture your server unnecessarily.

Advanced SQL Techniques: Cool Stuff when You Need It

★ UNION

★ Peg or display columns

★ Aliases

UNION

For some reason, many of the applications I've written have needed a UNION SQL statement. After I explained how to do them to my boss, he started using them like crazy. They saved him a lot of time doing the same processing manually by selecting into two grids, merging, and so on. You'll know if you really need to use one. A UNION operator joins the results of two SELECT statements, provided both statements have the same number of columns with the same data types.

I'll use a very paired-down version of the actual tables I've needed in the following example:

```
DATA_SMALL

KEY_ID     Integer

FLD_NAME   Char(20)

DATA_VL    Char(20)
```

Data:

KEY_ID	FLD_NAME	DATA_VL
1	EMP_NAME	Jones
1	TELE	908-999-1234

```
DATA_LARGE

KEY_ID     Integer

FLD_NAME   Char(20)

DATA_VL    Char(255)
```

Data:

```
KEY_ID     FLD_NAME    DATA_VL

1          COMMENTS    Long Comments

1          REASON      Long Reason
```

This was used in a system that created generic forms for data entry. A form could be created specifying fields defined in another program. All data was saved into two tables. Fields with a length of 20 or less went into DATA_SMALL; fields with a length over 20 went into DATA_LARGE. The problem was doing something like a report of all the data on a form. Since the data could be broken between these tables, two reports had to be generated, which was not desired. Instead a UNION was used to join the tables:

```
SELECT
        FLD_NAME, DATA_VL
FROM
        DATA_SMALL
WHERE
        KEY_ID = 1

UNION
SELECT
        FLD_NAME, DATA_VL
FROM
        DATA_LARGE
WHERE
        KEY_ID = 1
ORDER BY 1
```

The result is:

```
Col1       Col2

COMMENTS   Long Comments

EMP_NAME   Jones

REASON     Long Reason

TELE       908-999-1234
```

You get all the data from two tables retrieved in one statement. UNIONS can join more than two statements. One of my applications needs to UNION four statements together.

Two small important things about the UNION statement:

★ Notice that there is an ORDER BY with a UNION, but it doesn't specify the column by name. You must instead give the column position. Here the statement is ORDERED BY column 1 or FLD_NAME. Believe me, you will want your UNION statement ordered, and you won't know why your SQL won't run when you use the column name.

★ There is also a UNION ALL. A standard UNION statement eliminates any duplicate records in the retrieve. If both the tables in the preceding statements had a duplicate FLD_NAME, DATA_VL combination, only one of these records would be displayed. If you need to see duplicates records, then use a UNION ALL statement.

Peg or Display Columns

This brings up two new questions when using a UNION statement:
1. What if one table has a field you need retrieved but the other doesn't?
2. What if you need to know which table each record is retrieved from?

The answer to both is peg columns. I'm not sure what the standard SQL name for them is but that's what I call them. I have needed them in those four table UNIONS I was just babbling about.

Let's say the DATA_LARGE table has a field not in the other table:

```
EXTRA_FLD Char(20)
```

You still want to UNION the tables together, but you need the EXTRA_FLD field displayed for those records retrieved from the DATA_LARGE table. You also want a column that tells which table the record is from so your program can update the proper table with new information. This is exactly the situation I've encountered.

Here's the answer: SQL allows you to create a display column that is not associated with any column in the table. Any SQL manual will show you this in Chapter 1 or 2 but won't make it clear why you would really want to do this.

You can write senseless blather like:

```
SELECT
        'Employee Name Is' , L_NAME
FROM
        EMPLOYEE
```

Which returns:

Col1	Col2
Employee Name Is	Batters
Employee Name Is	Hanson
Employee Name Is	Whitworth

Not terribly useful but there it is in SQL Chapter 2. You really want to use this technique for situations like retrieving mismatched UNIONS and/or UNIONS where you need to determine a record's table of origin.

SQL based on the preceding senseless blather:

```
SELECT
        'DATA_SMALL', FLD_NAME, DATA_VL , ' '
FROM
        DATA_SMALL
WHERE
        KEY_ID = 1

UNION

SELECT
        'DATA_LARGE', FLD_NAME, DATA_VL, EXTRA_FLD
FROM
        DATA_LARGE
WHERE
        KEY_ID = 1
ORDER BY 1, 2
```

Returns:

Col1	Col2	Col3	Col4
DATA_LARGE	COMMENTS	Long Comments	AAA
DATA_LARGE	REASON	Long Reason	BBB

```
DATA_SMALL        EMP_NAME       Jones

DATA_SMALL        TELE           908-999-1234
```

The first column is a display column that shows the table of origin. SQL has no problem pairing up two display columns in the UNION statement. It also has no problem pairing up the display column, ' ' which is just a blank value with the EXTRA_FLD column, which is a character data type.

If EXTRA_FLD was a numeric, you would either:
1. Use a numeric display column

```
'DATA_SMALL', FLD_NAME, DATA_VL , 0

       (or if your SQL version will allow)

'DATA_SMALL', FLD_NAME, DATA_VL , NULL
```

2. Convert the numeric column to a string for display:

```
'DATA_LARGE', FLD_NAME, DATA_VL, CONVERT(CHAR, EXTRA_FLD)
```

Aliases

You need to use aliases in SQL when two or more of a table's fields need to be joined to the same field on a different table.

Example:

```
USER_RIGHTS

EMP_ID    Integer

LEVEL1    Integer

LEVEL2    Integer

LEVEL3    Integer
```

Data:

EMP_ID	LEVEL1	LEVEL2	LEVEL3
32000	4	2	1

```
RIGHTS

CODE      Integer

VALUE     Char(30)
```

Data:

CODE	VALUE
1	Read
2	Read/Write

```
3            Read/Write/Delete

4            Read/Write/Delete/Edit
```

Let's say you need to display the text value of a user's rights for a report. Each of the LEVEL fields value is in the RIGHTS table.

You cannot do this:

```
SELECT
        USER_RIGHTS.EMP_ID, RIGHTS.VALUE, RIGHTS.VALUE, RIGHTS.VALUE
FROM
        USER_RIGHTS, RIGHTS
WHERE
        USER_RIGHTS.LEVEL1 = RIGHTS.CODE AND

        USER_RIGHTS.LEVEL2 = RIGHTS.CODE AND

        USER_RIGHTS.LEVEL3 = RIGHTS.CODE
```

You'll get nothing back, since SQL is trying to find one record in RIGHTS where CODE simultaneously equals 4, 2, and 1.

You have do something like this:

```
SELECT
        USER_RIGHTS.EMP_ID, TABLE1.VALUE, TABLE2.VALUE, TABLE3.VALUE
FROM
        USER_RIGHTS, RIGHTS TABLE1, RIGHTS TABLE2, RIGHTS TABLE3
WHERE
        USER_RIGHTS.LEVEL1 = TABLE1.CODE AND

        USER_RIGHTS.LEVEL2 = TABLE2.CODE AND

        USER_RIGHTS.LEVEL3 = TABLE3.CODE
```

TABLE1, TABLE2, and TABLE3 are alias names for the RIGHTS table. SQL will treat this statement as if RIGHTS were actually three separate tables.

An alias is also used if you need to do a self-join, actually joining a table with itself. Here's a situation where you need to do a self-join:

```
KEY_TABLE

KEY_ID      Integer

FLD_1       Char(10)

FLD_2       Char(10)

FLD_3       Char(10)
```

Let's say the KEY_ID field will always be a unique value. You need to know whether any two records exist where FLD_1 = FLD_1, FLD_2 = FLD_2, and FLD_3 = FLD_3.

```
SELECT ONE.KEY_ID, ONE.FLD_1, ONE.FLD_2, ONE.FLD_3

    FROM KEY_TABLE ONE, KEY_TABLE TWO

WHERE

    ONE.FLD_1 = TWO.FLD_1 AND

    ONE.FLD_2 = TWO.FLD_2 AND

    ONE.FLD_3 = TWO.FLD_3 AND

    ONE.KEY_ID <> TWO.KEY_ID
```

The WHERE clause item **ONE.KEY_ID <> TWO.KEY_ID** ensures that you are not comparing a record to itself (since **KEY_ID** is unique), thus incorrectly retrieving all the records.

Cool stuff when you need it.

What Time Is It Mr. SQL?

Some SQL versions do not have separate data types for date and time. There may be only datetime and small datetime types. If you need to break up the datetime for display or comparisons, you can use the **CONVERT** function. Here's one example. Check your SQL manual for variations.

```
SELECT

    SELECT

    CONVERT(Char(10), BIRTH_DTTM, 101), CONVERT(Char(5), BIRTH_DTTM, 108)

    FROM

    EMPLOYEE
```

Returns:

```
Col1       Col2

12/01/1967  10:35
```

You might also need to display all the records for a specific date, regardless of time. This is common when generating reports. Your program might allow the user to enter a date in a text box or date VBX and then filter the report on this value. Make sure you convert any date value on the right-hand side of the equal sign to mm/dd/yyyy when using this SQL call.

This VB statement will convert the date in the text box **txt_date** to the desired format.

```
If IsDate(txt_date.text) Then

    txt_date.text = Format(txt_date.Text, "mm/dd/yyyy")

Else

    'Error Processing

End If
```

The SQL call:

```
SELECT

    L_NAME, F_NAME

FROM

    EMPLOYEE

WHERE

    CONVERT(Char(10), BIRTH_DTTM, 101) = '12/01/1967'
```

Nut House SQL *Nut House*

This section reveals a few subtle SQL problems I've encountered. When they happen, you assume you've finally gone nuts. First you start yelling at the monitor. Then you find another programmer, throw him or her in front of your computer and say, "Am I going crazy?" Here's a short list to consider when your SQL sends you over the edge.

Misunderstanding NULL SQL

The first problem is mistaking a field that is NULL for a blank field. Most versions of SQL allow a field to be declared NULL. If you never put anything in this field, it will remain NULL. However, when scrolling through the table, it looks just like a blank field. Your write the SQL call:

```
SELECT * FROM TABLE1

WHERE FLD1 = ''
```

and get either nothing or nothing close to the number of records that should be processed.

Then you write:

```
SELECT * FROM TABLE1
WHERE FLD1 = NULL
```

and, depending on your version of SQL, it still doesn't work. Problem number two.

Nothing equals NULL. For crying out loud, even NULL doesn't equal NULL. Remember, in some versions of SQL, either you IS NULL or you IS NOT NULL.

Finally, salvation:

```
SELECT * FROM TABLE1
WHERE FLD1 IS NULL
```

Test whether *field* = **NULL** works in your own version of SQL.

We also run into the same NULL problem with WHERE clauses expressing not-equal conditions.

```
SELECT * FROM TABLE1
WHERE FLAG <> 'Y'
```

This SQL will return all the records in which FLAG isn't equal to 'Y' but isn't going to get any of the records in which FLAG is NULL, since you really can't be equal or not equal to a NULL. To get this to work, you must include a NULL check in the WHERE clause:

```
SELECT * FROM TABLE1
WHERE (FLAG <> 'Y' ) OR (FLAG IS NULL)
```

Leading or Trailing Spaces/Case-Sensitivity

Does "aaa" = "AAA" ?
Does "a" = "a   " ?
Does "a" = "   a " ?

Any join or WHERE clause you write that incorrectly makes this assumption will reward you with no records. When in doubt, use the SQL functions to convert the fields to all upper- or lowercase, and trim any extraneous spaces. Be especially careful with fields that are a fixed-length character type. The value you save may automatically be padded with spaces. I needed to trim trailing spaces in a whole lot of SQL calls in one application. This was after I almost lost my mind wondering why a simple WHERE clause kept returning empty-handed. I kept rebuilding the index on the table, thinking it was corrupt. No such luck; I just didn't know what I was doing. I still told everyone it was a corrupt index anyway. They lie, I lie.

Wrong Field Linked in Join

This usually happens when SQL lines are cut and pasted together.

```
SELECT

        TABLE1.FLD5

FROM

        TABLE1, TABLE2

WHERE

        TABLE1.FLD1 = TABLE2.FLD1 AND

        TABLE1.FLD2=TABLE2.FLD2 AND

        TABLE1.FLD3=TABLE2.FLD2 AND

        TABLE1.FLD4=TABLE2.FLD4
```

To save time writing this SQL statement, I copied the first line and modified it. Unfortunately, I didn't change the third line correctly. I meant to join to TABLE2.FLD3. This problem can take a long time to discover in a large SQL statement.

SELECT DISTINCT

If SELECT DISTINCT is executed with an ORDER BY clause using a field not included in the retrieved column list, an erroneous return can result. This is an SQL problem on our Sybase Server. Maybe we just configured it wrong. Check if this situation occurs with your SQL database.

```
TEST Table

        FLD1      FLD2

        A         B

        A         C

        A         D
```

The SQL call:

```
SELECT DISTINCT FLD1 FROM TEST
```

Yields correct results: one occurrence of A in FLD1.

```
FLD1

A
```

However,

```
SELECT DISTINCT FLD1 FROM TEST ORDER BY FLD2
```

Returns:

```
FLD1

A

A

A
```

Clearly, this is not correct. A should only appear once. This is a sticky problem that can screw up your processing. Removing the ORDER BY clause will clear it up, but you'll lose your order. This problem caused a lot of pain in one of our applications. Try this example in your database. If it works, good; if not, then at least you have been forewarned.

Running Your SQL Pointing to the Wrong Database

I've done this several times and boy did I holler. This can happen when you change an INI file to another database and then forget to reset it. A stored procedure might be written hardcoded with an old database name. It's also possible that an attempt to connect to the database failed, so instead of being where you want, you end up in a default database.

Erroneous Results because the Index on the Table Is Corrupt

Data can seem to fall from the sky in this case. Actually, all the records are still there, but you need to re-create the index. I've found this problem mostly in dBASE tables. It's good DBA policy to regenerate indexes on heavily used tables on a regular basis.

Garbage Data

During development, programmers might test a specific program with dummy data loaded into the tables by hand. This data can have arbitrary key fields or lack support data in other tables. Be aware of who is in a test database and what tables they might be changing.

SQL Database Design *Database Design*

The actual design of the database is the one of the most crucial aspects of the application. It is not the job of the programmer (nor should anyone expect it to be) to establish the actual physical design of the system. This process should be done by a group of individuals who are experienced in both database design and the specifics of the industry and process that is being modeled. A hack programming job can be rewritten, but if you establish a physical design improperly, all the fancy programming in the world won't save the system.

The realization of faulty database design might begin as a vague feeling that the system isn't handling the process it was designed to perform. Patches are made to code and workarounds are established. Then, sometimes in one crushing blow, the system falls apart. The problem here is, unlike code that can be thrown away, you have real data either trapped somewhere it doesn't belong, or with nowhere to go in the first place.

The following section on normalization is meant as a programmer's eye view of the process and the effect it has on his coding. Please don't go out and design a complicated database using this information. Just act like a smart-aleck if you get to sit in on design phase meetings.

Normalization: Why Be Normal? *Why Be Normal*

One problem I find over and over again with systems development is that multiple copies of anything will, over time, fall out of sync. Whether it's programs on different servers, documentation on floppy and hard drive, or a group update to users' WIN.INI files, eventually you neglect one and it falls behind its siblings. At this point, feeling hurt and neglected, it begins jealously plotting revenge. Anyone who has been on the receiving end of this rage knows that it can be a cruel and agonizing fate. This is the real purpose behind database normalization.

Normalization solves the problem of sibling rivalry between data by enforcing strict population control. This is known as eliminating data redundancy. With no duplicates clamoring for attention, each data item is content and makes no attempt to fight the power.

A full treaty on normalization can and does take up entire books. Normalization is an art and a touchy subject. Pro and con arguments about the degree of normalization required flare up like the old Ford/Chevy debate. I don't view normalization as an academic exercise. I had one interview during which the guy proudly told me that all the company's database tables were normalized to the third form. All I care about as a programmer is that the data doesn't get duplicated all over the place. If that's the third form or the eighth form, then good. I don't pretend to understand all the normalization jargon (tuples?). My advice is simple: look at the data in the table that is not a part of the key; ask yourself, "If this data changed, how many places will I have to update it?" If the answer is more than one, then you've found a candidate for normalization.

In its most basic form, normalization is the process of going through your table design and isolating nonkey fields that can repeat duplicate information and putting them into a separate table. This table is then linked with the original table through key field(s).

Let's step through one normalization exercise using our Socratic method.

One-to-Many Relationships

Here's an unnormalized one-to-many relationship (actually this is Normal Form 1, which just doesn't cut it; unnormal is even worst than this):

```
EMPLOYEE Table

EMP_ID    F_NAME      L_NAME       START_DT       TELE_NUM

1         John        Capslock     12/01/1980     555-6234

1         John        Capslock     12/01/1980     555-5462

1         John        Capslock     12/01/1980     555-4552

2         Jane        Tonerlow     11/08/1982     555-3253

2         Jane        Tonerlow     11/08/1982     555-2234

...
```

This table allows an employee to have multiple telephone numbers, which are stored in the TELE_NUM field. However, all the other user data must be carried along to maintain the link with the employee.

Now ask the question: "If the L_NAME field for one employee changes, how many places will I have to update it?" It's not one. I don't like it. The solution is to break the table up and link it with the unique key EMP_ID field.

```
EMPLOYEE Table

EMP_ID     F_NAME        L_NAME          START_DT

1          John          Capslock        12/01/1980

2          Jane          Tonerlow        11/08/1982

...

EMP_TELE Table

EMP_ID     TELE_NUM

1          555-6234

1          555-5462

1          555-4552

2          555-3253

2          555-2234

...
```

If the primary key field EMP_ID did not exist, it would have to be added to the table. Now any change to L_NAME has to update only one record.

The primary key is one or more fields that establish the uniqueness of each row in a table. They are the backbone of normalization and relational database design used to establish relationships between tables. Primary keys are usually invisible to the user and always immutable. Change a primary key and you risk casting helpless orphan records into the cold database sea. If the EMP_ID field is changed accidentally in the EMPLOYEE table, any tables linked through this key would be lost.

One important thing to remember in any program that involves tables in a one-to-many relationship is that if the parent record is deleted, then the children records must also be deleted. Otherwise, you'll leave orphan records. If John Capslock goes, then his telephone numbers must go too.

Many-to-Many Relationships

Now that you're warmed up, let's jump into this classic table relationship, then cool down with a little one-to-one.

BOOK_STORE Table

STORE	ADDRESS	BOOK	PRICE
Rikki's Books	35 Oak St.	Bearded Spam	35
Rikki's Books	35 Oak St.	The Joys Of Ice	25
Rikki's Books	35 Oak St.	Onion Vapor	14
Mimi's Books	24 Elm St.	The Bearded Spam	35
Mimi's Books	24 Elm St.	The Joys Of Ice	25
Mimi's Books	24 Elm St.	Onion Vapor	14

...

In this relationship, each store carries many books, and each book is available in many stores. That's good for business but what a mess of a table we've got here. Let's ask the question: "If a single STORE field changes, how many places will I have to update it?" It's not one, is it? So let's break off the store and its related info into another table and add a key field.

STORE Table

STORE_ID	STORE	ADDRESS
1	Rikki's Books	35 Oak St.
2	Mimi's Books	24 Elm St.

That's nice. But we're not finished asking questions, are we? The other table now looks like this:

BOOK_STORE Table

STORE	BOOK	PRICE
1	Bearded Spam	35
1	The Joys Of Ice	25
1	Onion Vapor	14
2	The Bearded Spam	35
2	The Joys Of Ice	25
2	Onion Vapor	14

"If a single BOOK field changes, how many places will I have to update it?" It's not one, is it? Break it up boys. Take your friend PRICE along and slap an ID on it while you're at it.

BOOK Table

BOOK_ID	BOOK	PRICE
1	Bearded Spam	35
2	The Joys Of Ice	25
3	Onion Vapor	14

Now what do we have?

```
BOOK_STORE

STORE_ID  BOOK_ID

1         1

1         2

1         3

2         1

2         2

2         3
```

The result of our efforts is three tables instead of one. Now if we change the book name, the price, the store name or address, we only have to update one record in one table. Sweet. No tuples, no supersets, no extensions; just ask a simple question.

One-to-One Relationships: Lookup Tables for Limited Range Values

```
EMPLOYEE Table

F_NAME    L_NAME      DEPT

John      Caplock     Computer Information Systems

Jane      Tonerlow    Computer Information Systems

Sans      Serif       Finance

...
```

Imagine there are 10,000 employees in this company. 1,000 are in the Computer Information Systems department. DEPT is a 50-character field in the EMPLOYEE table. Your program displays the DEPT field value in a text box and saves the contents to this table.

You have two problems here:

1. If you make a typo spelling out Computer Information Systems, an employee record ends up in a phantom department all its own. A report based on the DEPT field will be incorrect.
2. Ask my question again. If Computer Information Systems changes to Information Services, as it did in my company, then you have to go in and change the DEPT field for 1,000 users. The person who will be assigned to do this will side with the jealous data when the rebellion breaks out.

Any field that has a limited range of values is a candidate for a lookup table. These include race, department, state, and country.

Here's what we do:

```
EMPLOYEE Table

F_NAME          L_NAME          DEPT_ID

John            Capslock        1034

Jane            Tonerlow        1034

Sans            Serif           1033

...


DEPT Table

ID    VALUE

...

1033  Finance

1034  Computer Information Systems

1035  Marketing

...
```

The DEPT field is replaced by a DEPT_ID field. This field does not store the actual department name. Instead it holds a pointer ID to another table. In this case, it's the DEPT table. Each ID field must be unique in the DEPT table for this to work.

The advantages of this design are as follows:

☆ The data redundancy problem is eliminated. A change to a department name now involves changing just one record. This can actually impress users. A system I just finished developing used a lookup table for the vendor name. The primary user of the system was hesitant about the maintenance task that was before her. A vendor had changed its name and she thought hundreds of records in the system would need to be updated. The ease with which the lookup table solved the problem impressed us both and won me over to normalization.

☆ The DEPT_ID can use a smaller field type to store this information than the original character 50. An integer value would work well in this situation. The result is a space saving, which could be considerable if the table has many records and long character fields.

The disadvantages of normalization (in this case and in general) from a programming perspective are:

★ The SQL gets more complicated. Before you wrote:

```
SELECT
        F_NAME, L_NAME, DEPT
FROM
        EMPLOYEE
```

Now:

```
SELECT
        F_NAME, L_NAME, DEPT.VALUE
FROM
        EMPLOYEE, DEPT
WHERE
        EMPLOYEE.DEPT_ID = DEPT.ID
```

This isn't a big deal here, but when a table has many lookup fields, you start wishing for the bad old days. The statement is harder to write and takes longer to execute. Remember SQL Error #1 when writing these statements.

★ The system must be able to generate these unique IDs. One of the first generic routines you'll need to write before you begin working with tables that have key ID fields is a function that will generate these IDs. There are several methods for doing this. They include:

Using random or semirandom numbers (not recommended).

Determining the highest ID currently in the table (probably by using the SQL call **MAX**) and incrementing it to get the new value.

Using a KEY_IDS table. Each key ID in the system would be one field or record in this table. Depending on how your system is set up, the table would look something like this:

KEY_IDS Table

EMP_ID	DEPT_ID	STATE_ID	COUNTRY_ID	RACE_ID...
1035	212	50	103	5

Or this:

```
KEY_IDS Table
KEY_NAME       ID
```

```
EMP_ID        1035
DEPT_ID       212
STATE_ID      50
COUNTRY_ID    103
RACE_ID       5
...
```

Your function would get the current value for the desired ID field, increment it, then update the KEY_IDS table with this new value. If this operation is successful, then you are guaranteed a unique ID. The function would return this ID to the calling program or return an error code if the operation was unsuccessful.

★ The programming to handle the ID/VALUE relationships can be hairy. I have to admit than when I was a strapping young buck I argued passionately against the ID/VALUE lookup table relationships in our applications. The reason is simple. From a programming perspective, this stuff is a real pain. Your form will display the lookup list using a drop-down combo box or some other control depending on your standards and preference. The user picks the Finance department. The program, however, doesn't save Finance to the DEPT_ID field. You need Finance's evil twin 1033.

Some add-on database controls perform ID/VALUE processing for you. You specify the lookup table, the display field, and the field that is actually saved. If you're not using such an add-on, or can't get yours to work properly, you'll have to do your own processing. However you handle this situation, standardize on one technique and have everyone use it. Otherwise, every programmer can and will reinvent the wheel with every program. The best bet, as always, is a set of generic global routines to help everyone out. I cover this in the "Data-Caching Techniques" section.

The Big SQL

The advantage of having a normalized database is that data redundancy is eliminated. The problem is that now everything is cloistered in its own little table. This is the counter-argument to normalization. Sure the data isn't redundant, but you gotta drive all over town just put it back together again.

As mentioned in the section "Normalization: Why Be Normal?" the joins just to get the lookup values can really fatten up your SQL call. Pulling all the data together in a complicated table relationship can result in an SQL whopper statement. In my current development environment, SQL joins of up to 13 tables are not uncommon. When you finally get one of these monsters to work, it's customary to run around and announce it like you just reeled in Moby Dick. "I just did an 11-table join! It almost killed me, but it's running now. I need an aspirin."

All the little SQL errors are magnified when writing Big SQL since there are so many places for things to go wrong. Every join and every condition is a potential cause of problems. If your big statement isn't working properly, go through it carefully looking for SQL Error #1 and #2 and all the Nut House cases. If it still won't work, then check with your project leader to see if you understand the table relationships properly.

Big SQL might also run extremely slow. Big and small SQL statements run much faster if you create them as a stored procedures. However, the dynamic nature of some SQL calls make this impossible. Stored procedures are not available in all versions of SQL. Also make sure your database add-on can execute them. Stored procedures should be included in the SQL scripts used to create a new database. (See the upcoming section "SQL Scripts: Play It Again, Sam.")

The other problem with Big SQL is that it just might be too complicated to run. I wrote a fancy-pants SQL statement with complicated nested SELECTS, UNIONS, and WHERE IN clauses and crushed the SQL server like an empty beer can. The poor thing collapsed in a heap and needed to be recycled. Now this is an extreme situation, but any big SQL call might cause problems or just run too slowly.

It's best to stress-test Big SQL in key program areas to see whether it will run when the tables have a belly full of data. What can happen is that everything runs okay when you're developing, but falls apart later on. Originally, the only records in the tables are some test data you added yourself. You can join a whole bunch of tables if they only have two records each. Once the tables get packed with data, it's another story. Sometimes it's best to write a stripped-down version of the original Big SQL call, then do additional calls for the other information.

To Proc or Not to Proc

As mentioned in the previous section, SQL runs faster as a stored procedure. The actual reduction in retrieval time depends on the complexity of the SQL statement. Unlike processing a raw SQL statement, when the server executes a stored proc, it doesn't have to compile and figure out the method it will use to get the desired records. The stored proc already has the road map the server will use to get the data to you. In a raw SQL call, it has to figure out the directions right then and there.

Some companies use nothing but stored procedures to process SQL. The most obvious reason is to increase performance and reduce the stress on the server. A server with large databases and many users is busy enough without having to thinking about how to process raw SQL statements. Additionally, stored procedures can act as a security system. If stored procedures are used for all SQL statements—including Inserts, Updates, and Deletes—then rights to perform these operations on the tables can be revoked from users. Users are granted rights to execute your application's stored procedures so they can process the data, but they can't sneak in the back door and poke around.

I use stored procs infrequently in my current development and really wouldn't want to go to the trouble of creating one for every SQL call I make. Some SQL statements just can't be converted into stored procedures. The other problem is that the statement itself is invisible. You just execute the stored proc to issue to call. If you've read the previous sections you've seen all the problems that can occur in a SQL statement. I'm the biggest fan of calling black-box generic routines, but I really want to see that statement. Having to create a separate stored procedure for every SQL statement in the project adds to development time and overhead. Fixing, recompiling, and retesting stored procs is a more complicated process than just changing an in-line SQL statement. Then again, probably once you're used to it you don't mind it as much, and you think all us randy, raw SQL boys are just a bunch of inefficient punk wannabes.

Vicious infighting aside, maintaining a stored proc library containing all the SQL calls for a large application is a full-time responsibility and as complicated and important as anything else in the development process. You better get a handle on this process or it's curtains for your applications. Sometimes there is an actual division of labor between the programmers, with some just doing the front-end processing and others just writing and creating the SQL stored procedures that these programs call to access data. I can only imagine the secret contempt these two teams have for each other.

The real issue here might be what is more important in your development environment: the processing time and efficiency of the server, or the coding time and efficiency of your programmers?

> Is it worth the extra development time and maintenance of stored procedures to reduce server overhead?
>
> Is it better to sacrifice some server time to ease programming headaches and reduce development time?
>
> Should complicated SQL statements even be issued, or should more basic statements be used with programmers performing additional processing at the client end?

This is the client/server dilemma. Whatever your company's decision, it will most likely be made by the big wheels and you'll just have to follow along grudgingly.

Concurrency and Data Integrity: Hey, I Was Here First!

Any system that will be used by more than one person at a time
(most on-line systems) should be concerned with data concurrency.
Here's the problem: One person retrieved a record for editing.
Another person goes in after this person, edits the same record,
then saves the changes. The first person now saves his or her
changes to the same record based on old data values. This wipes out
any changes the second person just made.

Example:

Mark and Kristara hold a join account at the company
store. You wrote a program that allows users to add funds
to this account electronically.
Mark goes into the program on his computer and retrieves
the join account record, **Rec ID = 15332**. The original
value in the ACCOUNT BALANCE field is $1,000.
Kristara then goes into the program on her computer just
after Mark, and retrieves the same account record.
Kristara adds $100 to ACCOUNT BALANCE then
updates the record.

```
ACCOUNT BALANCE = $1000 + $100          ($1100)

    UPDATE

        ACCOUNT_REC

    SET
```

```
                         ACCOUNT_BALANCE = 1100
             WHERE
                         REC_ID = 15332
```

*Mark now adds $200 to the old ACCOUNT BAL-
ANCE he retrieved, then updates the record.*

```
        ACCOUNT BALANCE = $1000 + $200          ($1200)
             UPDATE
                         ACCOUNT_REC
             SET
                         ACCOUNT_BALANCE = 1200
             WHERE
                         REC_ID = 15332
```

The total in the account should be $1300 ($1000 + $100 + $200). It
isn't, though, because Mark is working with outdated information.
Kristara changed the ACCOUNT BALANCE field since Mark
retrieved the record. Mark has just had the SQL version of a showdown with Dead-Eye Pete in "Overall Application Setup: Dodge
City." I'm a menace to society.

This is what we did in some of our applications to handle concurrency. Each table had an extra column called CSTAMP which was
type **tinyint** (0-255). The first SQL insert set this column to 0. The
CSTAMP was retrieved each time a record was retrieved and
edited. The program incremented the CSTAMP variable by one
each update, setting it back to 0 when it was at 255 (which would
certainly take awhile). The retrieved CSTAMP value was included
in the WHERE clause:

```
    UPDATE
            ACCOUNT_REC
    SET
            ACCOUNT_BALANCE = 1200,
            CSTAMP = 1
    WHERE
            REC_ID = 15332 AND
            CSTAMP = 0
```

If someone edited the record since you retrieved it, your SQL statement would fail because the CSTAMP was no longer the same. An

appropriate message could then be displayed to the user alerting him or her of this problem. This not necessarily the best or only solution; it was my idea after all. There are other versions of this scheme that use a larger CSTAMP field that stores more information, possibly the date, time, and user ID. The concept is still the same. If it's different from the value you retrieved, then somebody's been in there mucking around. My idea was used to save space. (You could cut it down even further, using Chr(1) and looping though 0-9.) Your SQL engine/database add-on may already handle concurrency either through record locking or its own timestamp system. Just make sure the issue is acknowledged and addressed before your application is developed.

Another technique to ensure data integrity is transaction processing. A group of SQL statements is all bundled up. This is a very tight-knit group that sticks together. If one member of the group fails to perform its operation, the others bail out too. This is how the conversation goes at the byte level: "If Johnny Update can't play, then none of us are playing. And guess what? We're taking back all the stuff we just did. Nyaaah, nyaaah, nyaaah!"

The method to do this varies, depending on your database add-on. Here's the process in general terms. A transaction is begun. A group of SQL statements is issued. If one of the statements fails, the entire group of statements is rolled back; otherwise, the results of all the statements are committed to the database.

This is necessary because certain SQL calls may be contingent on the success of others. Here's one example. If your delete of a parent record is successful but the subsequent delete of the child records fails, you're left with orphan records. Likewise, you don't want to insert child records if the insert of the parent record fails either. This violates a basic database rule: No children should be left unattended.

SQL Server Installation and Administration

In general, I think most computer training courses are lousy. Off with the lights, up with the transparencies, and down goes my head. The courses are usually all-day affairs, and I can't pay attention for more than an hour. Half the people taking the course, no matter what level, appear to have never seen a computer before. The one exception to this is a course that will train your SA/DBA to install and administrate your SQL server properly. My boss endured a week of these classes and returned with the realization that much of our current setup was inefficient or just plain wrong. This subject is just too arcane and important to be attempted with just a quick run-through of the manuals. A good course will allow you to avoid installation pitfalls and teach you how to tweak the server for maximum performance. You do not want to leave the server installation up to your rum-soaked brother-in-law just in from Connecticut on holiday.

Just as programmers shouldn't be expected to design the database structure, they shouldn't be expected to administer the database. You don't want every programmer running in and creating tables, rights, and user accounts on a whim. The responsibility for database administration should be established early. DBA duties vary from place to place but include handling user accounts and security, maintaining table indexes, and downing the server when necessary. The DBA should be responsible for ensuring that the databases—most important, those in production—are backed up. The restore procedure should be tested so you know that you'll be able to retrieve the old database if you need it.

Examine tools that will help in the administration process. You want the ability to maintain tables easily, run SQL scripts, and move easily between databases. A good Windows front end package is best. Otherwise you'll have to crawl around on your hands and knees in UNIX.

Everyone in the development group should at least know how to down and recycle the server. This is performed when the server crashes, which usually happens when all the grownups are out of town. The only troubleshooting/maintenance advice I can give is that if your database keeps a transaction log, check if it needs to be dumped periodically with the **DUMP TRANS LOG** command. If so, remember to do this on a regular basis or it will fill up at the most inconvenient time.

SQL Scripts: Play It Again, Sam

The SQL to create the tables for your application should be gathered together in one or more text files or scripts, which can then be used to generate a new database with ease. A problem with some new development groups is that they create the tables as they need them, slowly adding new tables into the database over time. I didn't believe this until I had an interview with a company that told me it did just that. Whenever a programmer felt the need for a new table, he or she just barged in and added it.

The problems with such a situation seem obvious:
1. Any future generations of developers looking at your application will have no way of knowing at a glance what tables are in the database.
2. If a new database needs to be created, someone will have to go through the entire old database, one table at a time, and try to reanimate it. I know because I had to do this with a legacy system at my current job. Luckily, there were only about five tables in the whole system, but this situation is intolerable. If there were 100 tables, the situation would be impossible (given my lack of patience).
3. A corrupted table might be lost to the ages. Trying to re-create it would be total guesswork. Pray that your backup system works.

These SQL scripts should reside in a subdirectory, probably named SQL, under the main application subdirectory.

```
\EMP
\EMP\SQL
\EMP\SQL\emp_sql1.sql
        \emp_sql2.sql
        \emp_sql3.sql
        \...
```

A further advantage of these scripts is that they act as a physical model of the database, a useful part of system documentation. I use the scripts as the basis for my Cradle to Grave variable names.

A sample script, **emp_sql1.sql**, might look something like this:

```
//Employee Database
//Tyrell Corporation
//12/01/1991
DROP TABLE EMPLOYEE;
CREATE TABLE EMPLOYEE
(USER_ID INTEGER,
LNAME VARCHAR(40),
```

```
FNAME VARCHAR(40),
MINITIAL CHAR(1) NULL,
EMP_NUM VARCHAR(5) NULL);


CREATE UNIQUE INDEX EMPLOYEE_IDX
ON EMPLOYEE (USER_ID );


GRANT ALL ON EMPLOYEE TO PUBLIC;
{continued on for all the tables in the system}

. . .
```

Any changes to the table structures should be made here in the script; don't just go in and alter the database. Update the table in the script, then create the new table using it. Otherwise, when you eventually use the scripts to generate a new database, your tables will go back in time.

SQL Cheat Sheet

I don't try to remember the proper structure or order of clauses in SQL. Neither should you. Create a SQL cheat sheet based on your flavor of SQL and the way your VB database add-on does its processing. Tack it on the wall. Add to the sheet as you discover any traps or tricks. My cheat sheet looks something like this:

```
SELECT [DISTINCT] col_list
FROM table_name
WHERE conditions
GROUP BY fld_name
HAVING
ORDER BY
COMPUTE row_agg(col_name)
BY col_name;
INSERT [INTO] table_name (col1, col2, col3, ...)
VALUES (data_value1, data_value2, data_value3, ...);
UPDATE table_name
SET col1=value1
```

```
        col2=value2

        col3=value3

WHERE conditions;

DELETE [FROM] table_name

WHERE search conditions;

GRANT ALL ON table_name TO user_name;
```

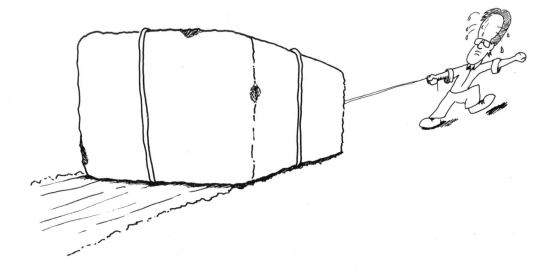

Standard File I/O: Dragging a Brick with a String

Although my current VB work uses a database add-on that allows me to access data using SQL calls, my original programming tasks were using good old flat-files processing based on the file I/O examples in the VB manual. You might as well work in COBOL on a mainframe. The processing is similar and very tedious. If you are planning to do any applications more complicated than a phone list, I encourage you to investigate the VB data control or database add-ons that will allow you to at least use SQL to talk to dBASE files.

I don't wish to waste your time showing you all the ridiculous things you must do to process data using standard VB calls to flat files. I saw a recent book on VB that devoted over 100 pages to flat-file processing. That awful link-list, queue, pointer garbage you had to learn in Computer Science 102. I never got past Computer Science 101 because my instructor insisted on singing during classes. The thought of taking another final while he dolefully chanted "Swing Low, Sweet Chariot" was more than I could take. However, since you may still need to maintain some legacy system, I offer the following:

★ If you must do flat-file processing, make sure you set up the application correctly. Build a firewall between the application project files and the data. Don't stick everything together. I've seen the data files for the application strewn throughout the application directory. Have a separate directory just for the data files, preferably on a network server that is backed up daily. (see "Back Up: You're Not My Type").

★ Don't hardcode the data path. Always make this a global variable. It's tempting to use no path at all, assuming the data will just sit right there in the same directory with the executable file. Don't build a system on a faulty assumption. (See "The Global Variable: Pathway to Exotic Locales" in Chapter 2.)

★ Use the **FreeFile** command to get the next available file number for **Open** commands. This ensures you won't pick a file number currently in use. An example of this is in the function **gfn_FileExists** in the section "The Mighty BAS," in Chapter 2.

★ Make sure that every file that is open is explicitly closed, especially if the data resides on a network. I've seen applications that ran fine on the local hard drive fail once they were copied to the network because the files weren't closed properly. Your local PC drive really doesn't care about file contention, but that's what network drives are all about. Forgetting to closing a file can cause real trouble.

★ Consider how much effort it would take to convert the application to run using SQL calls to real tables instead of using standard file I/O. The conversion will be painful, but you'll be rewarded later on with a faster, easier-to-maintain application.

PROGRAMMING TECHNIQUES

The following sections contain some programming techniques and idiosyncrasies I have used or encountered. It is an odd little collection of stuff. You can read about the basics of programming from the VB manual. I won't regurgitate it all here and waste your time. Much of what follows are warnings about danger areas or just personal favorite techniques and hangups.

Data-Caching Techniques

It is often necessary to retrieve data values for SQL processing yet not display this information to the user. Key ID fields and other secret information must be retrieved, but users often don't need to see, and certainly shouldn't be allow to change, these values. The following is a list of possible sneak fields you may need to hide from users' sensitive eyes.

Key Record IDs

In a normalized database, most tables are keyed on one or more unique ID fields. These ID fields are usually generated by the application itself and are meaningless to the user. Some users are actually frightened when they find out that a record's character and integrity are determined by an arbitrary but unique key ID value, not a text value that they typed in.

The Record's Original Field Values

These values are used when checking if changes have been made to the existing record or when audit trail processing is required.

Additional Sneak Fields

The following fields may also need to be squirreled away:

★ A timestamp field used in concurrency checking.

★ Record information fields: entry datetime, entry user, change datetime, special processing flags.

★ Sensitive information fields like salary.

Sneak field values can be hidden in various ways. I suggest you decide on a standard method for storing these values. Don't waste time tracking down the specific method you used in a project written six months ago. If possible, it's best to use the same technique to hide all the values. Data values can be hidden in form-level variables or assigned to an invisible control, most likely a text box or label. I again suggest using the Cradle to Grave naming technique.

Example: Storing the value for the field EMP_ID:

```
fs_EMP_ID = ffn_get_data()       'form-level variable

txt_EMP_ID.Text = ffn_get_data()  'text box with property Visible = False
```

(I'm using a function called **ffn_get_data()** to get the data item in several examples in this chapter. This is just a function made up for clarity. Your actual assignment method will vary.)

Records displayed in a grid can hide data fields by setting the field's column width to 1. The ideal would be to set the width to 0, but the grid doesn't agree with me.

```
grd_data.ColWidth(C_FLD_ID) = 1       'hide key column
```

A crafty user can still pull open the column and look at the goodies. If this is a sensitive data column, like salary, you can beef up security by putting the following code in the **MouseUp** event of the grid:

```
If grd_data.ColWidth(C_FLD_ID) > 1 Then       'some punk is trying
    ⇨to sneak a look see

    grd_data.ColWidth(C_FLD_ID) = 1  'rehide key column from
        ⇨prying eyes

End If
```

Otherwise, just let 'em look. Anyone patient enough to pull open a column with a width of 1 deserves something as a reward.

There is another interesting hiding place worth exploring. All objects have a property that's not used by VB and isn't displayed in the property box. This is the **Tag** property, and it's there just for you. Only you won't know this unless you managed to get up to the letter T in the manual without falling asleep. You can assign this property a string value up to 32K so you can use it instead of a variable to store a control's original value. The original value assigned to a control is necessary in order to be absolutely certain it has changed. Setting a flag variable in the **Change** event is no guarantee. A user can change a field, then change it back to the original value. Your application probably doesn't have to be this obsessive, but it's nice to know your options.

```
'Original Assignment
txt_name.Text = ffn_get_data()
txt_name.Tag = txt_name.Text

'Code Checking For Changes
If (txt_name.Tag <> txt_name.Text) Then
     MsgBox("Name field has changed. Can't save without your
        ⇨supervisor's approval.")
End If
```

Besides determining if a record has been changed, original data values might be needed for an application that must perform audit trail processing. This process involves recording any changes made to an existing record. Usually, a record is written to a separate audit trail table. This audit record can include fields listing the original data value, the new value, the user, date, time, and the reason for the change. This process may sound painfully tedious, and it certainly is. It's low-down, crawling-on-your-belly time. Audit trail processing makes my teeth ache. If you can't peer into the data grid or dynaset for the original values, then tags or form-level variables are the way to go. Please don't use a little of both. Trying to remember which values you assigned to tags and which to variables is a nasty waste of your time.

In addition to hiding data, we must also misrepresent it. A common process is data masking or code/value processing. The value dis-

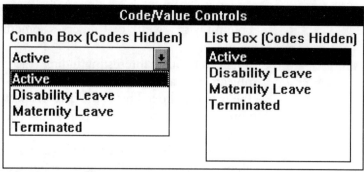

FIGURE 5.1 Code/value controls.

played for the field is not the same as the value saved in the data-base. Our record might have an integer STATUS_CD field that is represented using a drop-down combo box or list box (Figure 5.1). Its lookup table might look like this:

```
STATUS Table

CODE      VALUE

1         Active

2         Terminated

3         Maternity Leave

4         Disability Leave
```

A list of values from the lookup table STATUS is displayed in this control. The user picks the item Active, but instead of saving it as Active, it's saved by the code which is 1. Later on, when the record is retrieved, your program must set the display item based on this code. This whole process can be as bad as doing an audit trail. If you don't create a global function or set up a standard process for doing this, everyone will create his or her own technique. You don't want several flavors of this processing floating around. Assign this task to your best person and get a global routine going.

Any technique must do the following three things:
1. Load the control with the display/save data, showing only the display values. Ideally, the control and SQL statement are passed as arguments to a global routine.
2. Be able to set the display value based on a given save value.
3. Be able to return a save value given a selected display value.

You might have a third-party data-aware combo box that can per-form this masking technique. The display field and save field are set as properties. If this works, then you're in luck. I've never been blessed with any luck in programming. I always have to do everything the hard way. Let's look at the options.

The **ItemData** property can be used to store hidden values in a combo box or list box if this value can be expressed as a long integer. If you're hiding an alpha or alphanumeric value, you'll need another technique.

The code to load the control would look something like this (psuedocode is used because of undetermined access method):

```
Sub gsb_lst_load(a_ctl As Control, as_SQL_call As String)

    Dim ls_value As String

    Dim ll_code As Long

    'For Loop though a retrieved set of records from the lookup table
    'Assign the current record's code and value fields to the
        ⇨variables ls_value and ll_code

        'Add a value to the list box
        a_ctl.AddItem ls_value          'New value field is displayed

        'Assign the ItemData property for this value to the code
        a_ctl.ItemData(a_ctl.NewIndex) = ll_code        'New value
            ⇨field is hidden

'Loop back to next record in the set
End Sub
```

The following routine would set the display value based on a given code:

```
Sub gsb_lst_set_value(a_ctl As Control, al_code As Long)
    Dim li_ctr As Integer
    a_ctl.List Index = -1 'Deselect current item
    For li_ctr = 0 to (a_ctl.ListCount- 1)
        If a_ctl.ItemData(li_ctr) = al_code Then
            'Found Match - Select It
            a_ctl.ListIndex = li_ctr
            Exit For
        End If
    Next li_ctr
End Sub
```

The following routine would return the code for the currently selected item:

```
Function gfn_ctl_get_code (a_ctl As Control) As Long
    'Return the code for the display value
    If (a_ctl.ListIndex > -1) Then
        gfn_ctl_get_code = a_ctl.ItemData(a_ctl.ListIndex)
    Else
        'No Item Selected
        gfn_ctl_get_code = -1 'Or Some Other Error Code
    End If
End Function
```

The alternative to this technique is good old parsing. The value and code are added as one item. The code is shoved over with tabs or spaces. Since list and combo boxes don't have horizontal scroll bars, the code is effectively hidden. Unlike the **ItemData** technique, more than one value can be pushed off to the side, making it more versatile. You can go bananas in the global routine and allow any number of items to be hidden. Breaking up this orgy of data for processing is the tricky part.

Some unspeakable character must be placed between the values to separate them, something that the user can't normally type in. I've seen a lot of different methods, including using spaces to push the codes over, then using an unprintable character like Chr(1) for separators. One common method in a list box is to the use the tab character Chr(9). This will both shove the data over and act as a separator character when parsing things out. This won't work as well in a combo box since there the tab translates onscreen to a smudge, and thus the data doesn't move very far. You'll need put in many spaces first to hide the data, then the tab character.

Previous **gsb_lst_load** routine with different assignment line:

```
a_ctl.AddItem ls_value + Chr(9) + Trim(Str(ll_code))
```

The following routine would return the code for the currently selected item:

```
Function gfn_ctl_get_code(a_ctl As Control) As String
    Dim ls_item As String
    If a_ctl.ListIndex>-1 Then 'Item Selected
```

```
        ls_item = a_ctl.List(a_ctl.ListIndex)

        'Return the code for the display value
        gfn_ctl_get_code=Mid(ls_item, InStr(ls_item, Chr(9)) +1)
            ⇨'Take everything past the tab chr
    Else
        gfn_ctl_get_code=-1 'Or Some Other Error Code
    End If
End Function
```

The following routine would set the display value based on a given code.

```
    Sub gsb_lst_set_value(a_ctl As Control, as_code As String)
        Dim ls_item As String
        Dim li_ctr As Integer
        a_ctl.ListIndex=-1 'Deselect current item
        For li_ctr = 0 to (a_ctl.ListCount- 1)
            ls_item = a_ctl.List(li_ctr)
            ls_item = Mid(ls_item, InStr(ls_item, Chr(9)) + 1) 'Take
                ⇨everything past the tab chr

            If ls_item = as_code Then
                'Found Match - Select It
                a_ctl.ListIndex = li_ctr
                Exit For
            End If
        Next li_ctr

    End Sub
```

This is okay but remember that if the list box is wide, the tab character might not push all the items over far enough to hide them. Some will peer out ghoulishly from the right corner, ruining the illusion (Figure 5.2). You can use a combination of spaces and tabs, the number of spaces perhaps passed in as an argument to the routine. You can also set a tab stop greater than the Windows default for these controls using a technique that involves the API **SendMessage** call and some fancy footwork. It's a little hairy, and I don't want to add more confusion. Any API book will explain it to you. But I say, just convert it to a global routine instead of the rockhead form-level example the books will show you.

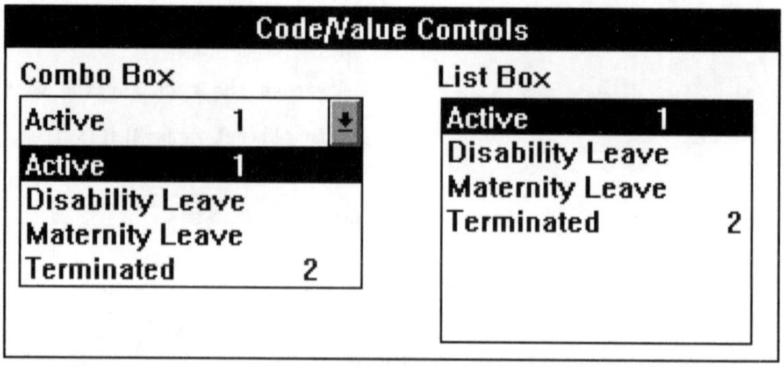

FIGURE 5.2 If not enough spaces are between the value and code, then you can see the wires, ruining the illusion.

The preceding example if good for hiding one valuc. If you do indeed decide to go bananas and hide multiple items, then more complicated parsing is required. Here's a generic routine that'll rip an item out of string:

```
Function gfn_return_item(Byval as_find_string As String,
    ⇨ai_find_element As Integer, as_chrs As String) As Variant

    Dim li_chrs As Integer

    Dim li_loc As Integer

    Dim li_len As Integer

    li_len = Len(as_chrs)        'Allow multiple character separator

    li_chrs = 1                  'If want the first item then ignore
                                    ⇨the loop


    Do While li_chrs < ai_find_element

        li_loc = InStr(as_find_string, as_chrs)

        as_find_string = Mid(as_find_string, li_loc + li_len)

        li_chrs = li_chrs + 1

    Loop

    If (as_find_string <> "" ) Then

        li_loc = InStr(as_find_string, as_chrs)

        gfn_return_item = Left (as_find_string, li_loc - 1)

    Else

        'Didn't find this item number - possible error
            ⇨msgbox situation

        'Just return blank for now

        gfn_return_item = ""
```

```
                End If
        End Function
```

Each item in the string is separated by one or more special characters. This string must also end with these special character(s) so the
last item can be parsed. You can use good old Chr(9) again or anything else, as long as the characters won't be part of any of the individual string items. This will screw things up. Example:

```
        Dim ls_text1 As String

        Dim ls_text2 As String

        Dim ls_item1 As String

        Dim ls_item2 As String

        Dim li_ctr As Integer

        ls_text1 = "a" + Chr(9) + "b" + Chr(9) + "c" + Chr(9) + "d" +
           ⇨Chr(9)

        ls_text2 = "a" + Chr(1) + Chr(9) + "b" + Chr(1) + Chr(9) + "c" +
           ⇨Chr(1) + Chr(9) + "d" + Chr(1) + Chr(9)
        'Loop through getting each item in the string
        For li_ctr = 1 to 4

           ls_item1 = gfn_return_item(ls_text1, li_ctr, Chr(9))
              ⇨'Chr(9) separator chr
           ls_item2 = gfn_return_item(ls_text2, li_ctr, Chr(1)+ Chr(9))
              ⇨'Chr(1) + Chr(9) separator chrs
           MsgBox(ls_item1)

           MsgBox(ls_item2)

        Next li_ctr
```

I hardcoded the values in **ls_text1** and **ls_text2** for clarity. They
could instead be assigned the selected item in list box, combo box,
and so on. This scheme allows you to use multiple characters to
separate items. Read the "Bad Characters" section later in this chapter before deciding on your secret go-between.

These are just the bare bones examples. You must figure out what
you need and are capable of with your own access method, and then
vigorously test your own global routines. Include error trapping,
comments and all that stuff. Once you're done, you'll be very happy.
I haven't written code/value processing in a long time. I have three
global routines that I call, and they handle everything I throw at
them. Write it once, then dance.

The KeyPress Edit Check: A Madman Seeks Revenge

Every VB programming book loves to give a variation on the following technique: It's just so easy to limit the user's input to a text box! Use that modern wonder, the **KeyPress** event. Look at what we do to allow only numeric entries in a text box:

```
Sub txt_numeric_KeyPress(KeyAscii As Integer)
    Select Case Chr$(KeyAscii)
        Case "0" to "9"

            'Accept Key
        Case Else

            KeyAscii = 0      'Reject Key
                Beep          'Annoy User
        End Select

    End Sub
```

Wow! Have a super day!

Usually, these schemes get incredibly elaborate, allowing backspaces, negatives, and decimal points. The listing scrolls on and on so proud it has made an impenetrable fortress against an onslaught of alpha characters. Now maybe those years as a grunt-level tester have left me cynical, but aren't they forgetting something? Go to the nearest regular text box. Select any of the data in its rich alphabet soup and copy it to the clipboard by pressing **Ctrl-Ins**. Now venture back to the numeric-only text box (Figure 5.3). Ready? Press **Shift-Ins**. What do you have now? The collapse of an empire. You can fill that sad little control with all the unspeakable text its **MaxLength** property will allow. Why doesn't anybody ever mention this? Well the dirty little secret is out. Just think, you can now invalidate 90 percent of the VB applications that are currently in production. Try this technique on a fancy custom VBX that only accepts numerics. Mine eats it up. I have a super-duper MaskedText VBX that GPFs when you paste invalid data into it. The tester has returned to seek his revenge.

Now what should you do while I'm busy plotting to take over the world? Put the following code in the **KeyDown** event of the text box.

```
Sub txt_numeric_KeyDown (KeyCode As Integer, Shift As Integer)

    If (KeyCode = KEY_INSERT And Shift = 1) Then 'Shift-Ins
      ⇨Pasting From ClipBoard

        'Type Keystrokes Into Control Thus Triggering KeyPress
          ⇨Event And Edit Check

        SendKeys ClipBoard.GetText()

    End If

End Sub
```

When users do a **Ctrl-Ins**, they are copying a value to the clipboard. **Shift-Ins** then pastes this same value from the clipboard to the active control. This is a powerful feature of Windows. It usually saves time and typos. What it doesn't do is trigger the **KeyPress** event. Our little subroutine simply takes the contents of the clipboard and types it into the control one character at a time. Now the **KeyPress** event can leap into action and halt the offending characters.

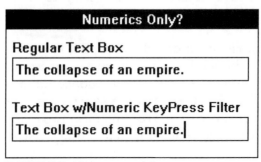

FIGURE 5.3 Numerics only?

Of course we are not quite finished. There's always more than one way to do everything in Windows. This is what makes users nuts. You can also paste information into a control by typing **Ctrl-V**. This is trapped in the original **KeyPress** event. It's likely your edit check inadvertently traps and disregards this as a special character, but you better go test it. Here's an example that lets **Ctrl-V** do its stuff without messing things up.

```
Sub txt_alpha_KeyPress (KeyAscii As Integer)
    'Good old Select Case statement.
    Select Case KeyAscii
        Case 22 'Pressed Ctrl-V
            KeyAscii = 0    'Throw Away The KeyStroke
            'Type Keystrokes Into Control Thus Triggering
                ⇨KeyPress
            'Event And Edit Check
            SendKeys Clipboard.GetText()
        Case Else
            'Whatever Normal KeyPress Stuff You're Doing
            KeyAscii = Asc(UCase(Chr(KeyAscii)))
                ⇨'Convert To All Caps
    End Select
End Sub
```

Now, I'm being nice here in these examples, converting and processing the paste of data. The important thing is to prevent bad data from getting into the field. If you don't want users to be able to paste information into a control at all, then just set the **KeyCode** or **KeyAscii = 0** where I use the **SendKeys** command and stop that data cold.

I suggest you write a global routine to process the **Shift-Ins** in **KeyDown**. You can put it in the MASK.BAS that contains all the different **KeyPress** edit checks. Remember to include the **Ctrl_V** check in any global **KeyPress** routines included in this BAS file.

You can perform this data paste processing on the form level. First, write another global routine to process **Ctrl-V** in the **KeyPress** event. These two global routines can then be called from the form-level **KeyPress** and **KeyDown** events. Set the form's property **KeyPreview = True** and these two calls will take care of all the controls on the form. The world is safe once more.

Curses, my plans have been thwarted by three lines of code!

Bad Characters

We just looked at how we can make a mess by putting invalid data into a field. While we are on the topic of destroying Windows applications, here are a couple of characters we can count on to join in the fight. If we can sneak these into an unsuspecting data field or string variable, we might gum up the works some more.

Here are a few of the local hooligans and their MOs.

Chr(0): null

Chr(0) behaves himself when he's in a string variable but has the nasty habit of eliminating anybody who is waiting behind him when this string is assigned to a control. Try the following example:

```
Dim ls_char_test As String

ls_char_test = "Where " + Chr(0) + "oh, where, did the data go?"

txt_char_test.text = ls_char_test    'Assign string to a text box
```

```
MsgBox (ls_char_test)                    'Display string in a message box

lst_char_test.AddItem ls_char_test  'Add string to list box

grd_char_test.AddItem ls_char_test  'Add row to grid
```

If you look at the value of **ls_char_test** in the debugger you'll see Where {smudge}oh, where, did the data go? but nothing after the **Chr(0)** will display in any of the assignments. If you needed that data, then you're in trouble.

API calls that accept and modify strings put the null character into these strings. If you declare a fixed length string, then it's initialized to nulls. If you never assign anything to this variable, it will stay that way. That cute little nullie was ruining the logic in one of my programs until I finally caught on.

The following code will not put up the message box because the value is null, not blank:

```
Dim ls_fixed_string As String * 1


If Trim(ls_fixed_string) = "" Then

     MsgBox("The string is blank.")

End If
```

Chr(9): Tab

This is the handy little guy that we used earlier to separate data in a list or combo box. An entire multicolumn record can be added to a grid if the fields are separated by Chr(9):

```
grd_test.AddItem "one" + Chr(9) + "two" + Chr(9) + "three" + Chr(9)
  ⤷+ "four"
```

Unfortunately, if Chr(9) is one of the characters in a field's actual data value, he destroys both of these schemes. The parsing search may now return the wrong value, and the grid **AddItem** command will put data in the wrong columns. You won't realize there's a problem until it's too late, especially if these values or columns are hidden from view.

Chr(9) usually can't be entered as data in a text box by pressing the **Tab** key since VB will just jump out of the control. Not always, of course. Here's a little stunt that just screwed up one of our data export programs. If a text box has **MultiLine = True**, and there are no other controls on the form with a **TabStop = True**, then you can't jump to another control. You just sit there, press **Tab**, and shovel in the Chr(9)s. Also, a Chr(9) can get pasted into a regular text box from another source or assigned from code. You won't see it, but it will be there waiting to ruin your day.

Chr(13) + Chr(10): Carriage Return Line Feed

These two thugs are able to throw data over to the next line. This is what happens when you press the **Enter** key in a text box with the **MultiLine property = True**. Nothing wrong with that, but Chr(13) can mess things up if you use the **Clip** command to assign data into a grid. The **Clip** command works on the currently selected area of a grid. You can determine the contents of, or assign values to, the region. When assigning a group of data elements to the grid in this manner, our old friend Chr(9) indicates a new cell in the row and Chr(13) indicates the beginning of a new row. If you have a Chr(13) embedded in an actual field value, then you're going to have a first-class mess. Data will end up in the wrong row, wrong column, and who knows what else. The grid can be a dangerous zone if any of the characters mentioned in this section sneaks in.

These are the characters and situations that I know have caused problems at one time or another. They might also cause problems in other objects (VBXs) depending on how they process data. I'm sure there are other characters that are little monsters that I haven't run into yet. Your application might run fine with certain weird characters, but later on they may cause problems. Perhaps your data is exported to another platform or system, such as SAS, for statistical analysis. If that other system starts barfing on the data, it's time to start hunting for those invisible invaders.

You might write a global routine like the following to remove offensive characters from strings where you know they might cause problems. This function removes all occurrences of the character.

```
Function gfn_remove_bad_chrs (as_data As String, as_bad_chr As
 ⇨String) As String

    Dim li_char_loc As Integer

    Dim li_char_len As Integer

    Dim ls_new_data As String


    ls_new_data = as_data      Original value passed to the routine
```

```
li_char_len = len(as_bad_chr)     'Can Be Mutiple Characters

li_char_loc = InStr(ls_new_data, as_bad_chr)     'Look for bad
   ⇨character


Do While li_char_loc <> 0     'Keep looking until all bad
   ⇨characters are found

    'Remove bad character from the string

    ls_new_data = Left(ls_new_data, (li_char_loc - 1)) +
       ⇨Mid(ls_new_data, (li_char_loc + li_char_len))

    li_char_loc = InStr(ls_new_data, as_bad_chr)   'Look for
       ⇨another bad character

Loop


gfn_remove_bad_chrs = ls_new_data     'Return string without
   ⇨bad characters


    End Function
```

If we add a call to this function in our first example, everything should turn out O.K.:

```
ls_char_test = gfn_remove_bad_chrs(ls_char_test, Chr(0)) 'Remove
   ⇨all instances of Chr(0)

'. . . the rest of the code
```

In this function, the **as_bad_chr** argument can be multiple contiguous characters, so you can strip out the carriage return line feed from a string. I had to do this in a program shortly after I finished this chapter.

```
ls_char_test = gfn_remove_bad_chrs(ls_char_test, Chr(13) + Chr(10))
   ⇨'Remove CR-LF
```

Now, I know what you're thinking. Why am I doing all this? Am I just obsessing over something stupid again? I don't doubt it. I've never claimed to be in good mental health. However, there may come a time in the history of your application when someone will innocently paste data into a field from another source and a weird character will come along for the ride. Your SQL tables might be prefilled with data or import it from another source. Who knows what might come traveling in on a DDE link? I sure don't, because I can never understand the examples enough to try it.

If you have a code scheme that relies on this character for special processing like the parsing algorithms in "Data-Caching

Techniques," or it is used by a VB control itself as in the previous examples, then you're going to have a bug. A bug that by its unprintable nature will be invisible to the eye. Nothing will be wrong in the code. The system may have worked perfectly for 10 years. It might take you three weeks to track it down, and then you're going to jump out the window. This may never happen to you (I hope) but I figured I'd send out a hysterical warning message anyway. This problem has happened to me more than once. Everything's fine since I'm on the first floor and the windows don't open.

No Comment

I'll give you the standard party line. Use comments throughout your code. Ask yourself whether you'll be able to understand what you just did six months from now. When in doubt, put in too many; later on, you'll be glad you did.

Visual Basic makes in easy to put comments in your code. You can use the good old REM statement or the faster shorthand of the single quote. Unfortunately, the process of commenting code is often neglected during development. Programming, especially difficult passages, is absorbing. Stopping to add comments breaks your concentration. The problem is that, when you look at your brilliant work later on, you may have no idea what inspired such musing. As a maintenance programmer you may look at a tangle of code that seems irrelevant, not realizing there is some vital process contained within the mess. Anything weird you must do as a workaround should be commented. Usually, these comments are filled with pathos:

```
'The next line of code is needed or the programs crashes. Why? I
⇨don't know. I hate this job.
```

Proper comments can help make generic routines understandable upon first reading. This is very important to the global BAS files you will be building for your projects. The purpose of the routine should be apparent after reading through the opening comments. You don't want to have to track down the author to explain it. Include the standard comment header described later in this section. Also include a description of any argument variables passed to the routine. If the routine is a function, then explain what the possible return values are and what they mean. We all get lazy putting comments in our everyday code. Just don't get lazy in a global routine.

Example:

```
Function gfn_check_for_chr (as_data As String, as_chr As String) As
   ⇨Integer

     'Arguments

     'as_data      - string to be processed

     'as_chr       - character to search for


     'Function returns Integer

     '-1 (True) Found the character in the string

     '0 (False) Didn't find the character


     'Programmer's Name:   Mark Warhol

     'Purpose:             Search for a specific character in a
                              ⇨string

     'Date:                12/01/1993

     'Revision History:


     '. . . the rest of the code
```

A good commenting practice is to include headers on all your code modules (subroutines, functions, events). Include at least:

```
'Programmer's Name:   Mark Warhol

'Purpose:             Export to ASCII File

'Date:                12/01/1991

'Revision History:    Mark Warhol - 12/14/1991 - Fixed bug when 0
                         ⇨records retrieved
```

This way, maintenance programmers know what they're up against even before looking at the actual code: "Uh. Oh. Warhol wrote this. He was the worst programmer who ever lived. I hate his coding style. What kind of moron feels possessed to use an underscore in all his variable names? Hey, he still owes me $11 for his farewell lunch."

" 'Export to ASCII File.' Well at least I know what the poor idiot was trying to do. Written in 1991. Hmmm, we've had a VB upgrade since then and now use a lot more global routines. He must have a lot of junk in here. I see he had to fix at least one bugaroo. Probably forgot to mention the hundred other ones. I'll just gut this sucker and start over from scratch."

I know this will happen. That's probably why I'll never leave my present job. The thought of countless generations of programmers laughing at my code is just too great to bear.

LostFocus/GetFocus: Get Like You Was before You Got Like You Is

You should be wary of any code in a control's **lostfocus** or **getfocus** event. Seemingly bizarre problems can result, especially if the code in these events is used for conditional navigation. The big problem is trying to set focus to a specific control from a **lostfocus** event.

Let's try a simple example to show what can happen. We have a form with two text boxes named txt_one and txt_two, and one command button named **cmb_save** that will save the data in these two fields. The tab stops are 0, 1, and 2 respectively.

Here's the processing: Txt_one and txt_two are required fields. The required processing is that the user can't tab off either field unless a value is entered. Otherwise a warning message box is displayed and focus must remain on the current field. Hey, that's easy. This'll just take a sec. Let's write a few lines of code and break for lunch.

```
Sub txt_one_LostFocus()

    If Trim(txt_one.Text) = "" Then

        MsgBox("Txt_one is a required field.")
```

```
                    txt_one.SetFocus              'Don't let user leave the field
          End If
     End Sub

     Sub txt_two_LostFocus()
          If Trim(txt_two.Text) = "" Then
               MsgBox("Txt_two is a required field.")
               txt_two.SetFocus              'Don't let user leave the field
          End If
     End Sub
```

Go ahead and try it. Leave **txt_one** blank and press the **Tab** key (Figures 5.4a and 5.4b). I'll wait . . . .

How's it going? Going so well it'll never stop. Good old infinite loop processing. Press **Ctrl-Break** before you lose your sanity. And remember, the users won't have this option. They'll have to do a **Ctrl-Alt-Delete**, and they won't be happy about it.

Let's try another example to show a more subtle problem that can happen using conditional **lostfocus** processing. We have a form with four text boxes: txt_one, txt_two, txt_three, and txt_four with tab stops 0, 1, 2, and 3 respectively.

Here is the special logic the screaming users demanded:

If txt_one is empty then
            lostfocus should set focus to txt_three

If txt_two is empty then
            lostfocus should set focus to txt_four

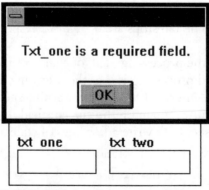

FIGURE 5.4A LostFocus example Ia.

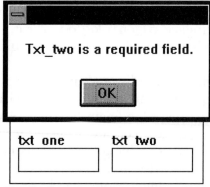

FIGURE 5.4B LostFocus example 1b.

The code again seems trivial:

```
Sub txt_one_LostFocus()
    If Trim(txt_one.Text) = "" Then
        txt_three.SetFocus
    End If
End Sub

Sub txt_two_LostFocus()
    If Trim(txt_two.Text) = "" Then
        txt_four.SetFocus
    End If
End Sub
```

Give it a whirl. Leave txt_one blank and press the **Tab** key. Does it jump to txt_three like a good little cursor? Of course not.

The same thing is happening in both these examples. A **lostfocus** event means just that. It's triggered when you're not there anymore. Some other control must have focus if a **lostfocus** event is triggered. If this other guy has any code in the **gotfocus** or **lostfocus** event, you may be in for a world of hurt.

In the first example, the **lostfocus** event in txt_one is triggered after focus has shifted to txt_two. The code in txt_one's **lostfocus** event attempts to set focus back to txt_one. However, any code in txt_two's **getfocus** event gets executed after txt_one's **lostfocus** event. There isn't any code here, so we're safe so far. But setting focus back to txt_one then triggers the **lostfocus** event in txt_two since it's now the control that has focus. Well guess what? This triggers the lostfocus event in txt_two. It sets focus back to txt_two. Which triggers txt_one's lostfocus event, which sets focus back to txt_one. These two will battle it out until the sun goes cold.

That's the awful reality. A control's **lostfocus** event is not the place to try to set focus to another field, even back to itself. The field that the cursor jumped to originally will have its **getfocus** event triggered. When your code explicitly sets focus to another field, the **lostfocus** event of this new current field will also get triggered.

The second example shows this clearly. Txt_one's **lostfocus** event attempts to set focus to txt_three. What happened? The event was triggered when you tabbed off to txt_two. When you set focus to txt_three, the **lostfocus** event in txt_two was executed, which set focus to txt_four. Not nearly as deadly an error but certainly not the result we had hoped for.

To get a better handle on all that's going on in the second example, add a list box to the form. In each **getfocus** and **lostfocus** event add an item to the list box that says that the event was processed.

After tabbing off of txt_one the list box will have the items shown in Figure 5.5. Whole lotta events going on. Put conditional code behind each one and who knows what'll happen.

Usually, everyone learns this one the hard way. First they promise someone an elaborate field-level validation scheme. Then they wonder what on earth is going wrong. Well there it is. Windows programming. Events trigger when you don't want them. They don't trigger when you do. Absolute agony.

```
┌─────────────────────────────────────────────────┐
│              LostFocus Example#2                │
├─────────────────────────────────────────────────┤
│                                                 │
│  txt one        txt two      Events Triggered   │
│  ┌──────────┐   ┌──────────┐ ┌────────────────┐ │
│  │          │   │          │ │txt_one GotFocus│ │
│  └──────────┘   └──────────┘ │txt_one LostFocus│ │
│                              │txt_two GotFocus│ │
│  txt three      txt four     │txt_two LostFocus│ │
│  ┌──────────┐   ┌──────────┐ │txt_three GotFocus│ │
│  │          │   │▏         │ │txt_three LostFocus│ │
│  └──────────┘   └──────────┘ │txt_four GotFocus│ │
│                              └────────────────┘ │
└─────────────────────────────────────────────────┘
```

FIGURE 5.5 LostFocus example 2.

What we really need is a different event. An event that would solve a lot of problems would be the I'm_Just_About_To_LoseFocus_ Tell_Me_What_Control_Is_About_To_GetFocus_But_Don't_Go_ There_Unless_I_Say_So event.

So what can we do about any of this? The easiest thing is to get frightened out of your wits by the examples and don't try any of this fancy stuff. Tell your dopey project leader it's a bad idea. I unfortunately did have to do this processing on a generic data entry form. Conditional tabbing, checking values at the lostfocus event, the works. The program is slowly draining the blood from my veins. Let's convert the first example to a method somewhat similar to what I had to use.

This example uses form-level events only:
1. Set all controls on the form to **TabStop = False.**
2. Set the form's **KeyPreview = True.**
3. Assign tags to each control so you can figure out which control has focus using the **ActiveControl** command:
   txt_one.Tag = "txt_one"
   txt_two.Tag = "txt_two"
   cmb_save.Tag = "cmb_save"
4. Form-level code.

```
Sub Form_KeyPress(KeyAscii As Integer)

    'Throw away this keystroke - everything is processed in the
      KeyDown event

    'If this is not thrown away the Shift-Tab will not work

    If KeyAscii = KEY_TAB Then

        KeyAscii = 0

    End If

End Sub

Sub Form_KeyDown(KeyCode As Integer, Shift As Integer)


If KeyCode = KEY_TAB Then

    Select Case Screen.ActiveControl.Tag   'I'd like to use just
        ⇨Screen.ActiveControl

                                            'but it didn't work

        Case "txt_one"    'Don't losefocus if blank

            If Trim(txt_one.Text) = "" Then

                MsgBox("Txt_one is a required field.")
```

```
                Else
                        If Shift = 1 Then
                                'BackTab
                                cmb_save.SetFocus
                        Else
                                'Tab
                                txt_two.SetFocus
                        End If
                End If
        Case "txt_two"  'Don't losefocus if blank
                If Trim(txt_two.Text) = "" Then
                        MsgBox("Txt_two is a required field.")
                Else
                        If Shift = 1 Then
                                'BackTab
                                txt_one.SetFocus
                        Else
                                'Tab
                                cmb_save.SetFocus
                        End If
                End If
        Case "cmb_save"     'No special processing
                        If Shift = 1 Then
                                'BackTab
                                txt_two.SetFocus
                        Else
                                'Tab
                                txt_one.SetFocus
                        End If
        End Select      'Case Screen.ActiveControl.Tag
End If 'KeyCode = KEY_TAB
End Sub
```

That's right, you have to crawl on your belly to get this to work.
Setting **TabStop = False** for all controls allows us to trap for Tab at
the form-level key events. Otherwise, it won't get processed. Here
we must check the state of the field, then set focus if all is well. Oy.

Of course, there's still a problem. You can evade our little scheme by using the mouse to click on another control. Unless we take the user's mouse away, we've got a hole in the fence here. Maybe there's a way to prevent the mouse from clicking and setting focus on another field. I don't know how to do this. Maybe by using some gizmo from API land.

This is a problem even using a standard **lostfocus** scheme. You can jump over a hundred required or special process fields and press the **Save** key by using the mouse. If you only do a validity check at the **lostfocus** event for a field and it never gets focus, then this check never get performed.

As a result, we need to put an additional check in the **click** event of cmb_save to see if either of the two fields is blank. If so, then we put up a message box and don't save the data.

```
Sub cmb_save_click

    Dim ls_msg As String
    Dim l_ctl As Control

    If Trim(txt_two.text) = "" Then
        ls_msg = "txt_two"
        Set l_ctl = txt_two
    End If

    If Trim(txt_one.text) = "" Then
        ls_msg = "txt_one" + Chr(13) + Chr(10) + ls_msg
        Set l_ctl = txt_one
    End If
    If ls_msg <> "" Then
        MsgBox("Required field(s) missing. Please enter: " +
            ⇨Chr(13) + Chr(10) + ls_msg)
        l_ctl.SetFocus
    End If

    'Continue on to save processing . . .
End Sub
```

I suggest that you just have this check at the **save** event (since you'll need it no matter what) and forget about the additional **lostfocus** processing. This will save you a lot of hassle.

Here's another reason why you need to recheck field values at the **save**. Make another test form. Include a text box and a command button, named txt_one and cmb_save respectively. Add the following code:

```
Sub txt_one_lostfocus
    If Trim(txt_one.Text) = "" Then
        MsgBox("Txt_one is a required field.")
        txt_one.SetFocus
    End If
End Sub


Sub cmb_save_click
    MsgBox("Just perform save processing, don't recheck txt_one.")
    'Rest of the save processing
End Sub
```

Now run this one. Press the command button. The command button doesn't put up its message box, so its event isn't getting triggered. The **lostfocus** event in txt_one is get processed. Very good. Not an elaborate setup but it's working. Now set the caption in the command button to include an access key. Try **&Save**. Now run it again. Is the focus on txt_one? Press **Alt-S** to save. What happened? The **click** event of the save button got executed but the **lostfocus** event in txt_one wasn't. Ha! We can avoid the **lostfocus** processing if we use the access key. Pretty slick, huh? Remember the **lostfocus** event doesn't get triggered if you click on a menu item either. Will the agony ever end?

Here's another annoying thing that will happen with **lostfocus** event processing. Add another command button called cmb_exit to this new test form with this code.

```
Sub cmb_exit_click
    End        'Just Quit
End Sub
```

Now run it. With focus on txt_one, press the **Exit** command button. You get the required field message box. Hey, you don't care about required fields, you're trying to exit the form. The **lostfocus** event doesn't know you're just trying to exit.

Remember the event we really wanted: I'm_Just_About_To_

LoseFocus_Tell_Me_What_Control_Is_About_To_GetFocus_But_
Don't_Go_There_Unless_I_Say_So.

If we had that event in txt_one, we could check if focus had
switched to the Exit button and disregard our edit check. But it ain't
there, and we're stuck.

I think I've picked on poor old **lostfocus** event enough. I suggest
you write my fantasy event on an index card and tack it on the bulletin board next to the picture of Betty Page. Whenever you write
any code in the **lostfocus** event, reread that card. Ask yourself
whether your code actually needs to be in this event to work properly. Remember, Miss **Lostfocus** is not your fantasy girl.

Here's one more situation that can get us into trouble. If code in an
event ends up triggering this same event, then you get an infinite
loop. The active, change, resize, or getfocus events are possible danger areas. Different places, but essentially the same problem. I'll
cover one; the rest follow the same pattern. The lazy, lunatic users
don't want to press a command button to launch a popup form.
Instead, when they tab to a certain control, say txt_one, they want
this popup form to come up automatically.

```
Sub txt_one_getfocus

        frm_popup.Show MODAL

End Sub
```

You know what happens. The user tabs to txt_one. The **getfocus**
event is triggered, displaying a popup form. The user does some
processing on frm_popup, then presses this form's **Exit** command
button. Focus now returns to txt_one on the calling form, and we're
at it again. No exit. Infinite reoccurrence of the same.

Yes, it's as bad as Nietzche said it would be. Hey, It's not too late to
switch into marketing—tasseled loafers, meaningless buzzwords, cute
girls will talk to you. Anyway, if you really need to do something like
this, here's a kludgy fix that will solve the infinite looping problem.

```
Sub txt_one_getfocus

        Static li_ignore_event As Integer       'Static local variable
            ⇨maintains its value

                                    'after routine is completed

        If li_ignore_event = False Then    'Event wasn't triggered by
            ⇨its own processing
```

```
                li_ignore_event = True    'The event will trigger itself
                    ⇨so set this flag to true

                                          'Then the processing won't get
                    ⇨redone and infinite loop
                'Do the specific event-level process
                frm_popup.Show MODAL
            Else
                'This event triggered itself
                'li_igore_event = True - bypass the processing but reset
                    ⇨flag so
                'the next time the event will be processed
                    li_ignore_event = False
            End If
        End Sub
```

This code bypasses the processing if the event has been triggered by itself. Ugly but it works. I've needed to use it several times.

I guess you can tell I hate conditional event processing. Don't get turned off because I'm a grumpy old man. I just want you to have an understanding and respect for the problems inherent in event-driven processes. Unfortunately, this "it should happen automatically" garbage always gets me in trouble. I would prefer requiring the user to press a command button and then launch whatever processing was originally put behind these sexier events. Then again, I also eat my morning roll without butter.

Calling Another Form's Routine: You Can't Get There from Here

You can't call a subroutine or function on one form from another. If you have a project with multiple forms that perform similar processes, then any common routines or variables should be written in a BAS file. However, sometimes some of the processing on a single form is later broken into several forms, and moving and converting the routine(s) and variables might be tricky. When the gurus in my development lost their minds and decided to convert everything to MDI parent-child forms, I used the following kludgy technique.

If you really need to perform a routine on, say, **form_main from frm_detail**, then you can put the actual call to this routine in the

click event of an invisible command button on **frm_main**. Execute this call from **frm_detail** by setting the command button's value to 1, which clicks the button.

Code on the **frm_detail** form:

```
frm_main.cmb_recalc.Value = 1              'Click button on other form
                           'you can't call frm_main.cmb_recalc_click
```

Code in the command button on the **frm_main** form:

```
Sub cmb_recalc_click()

      Call fsb_recalc

End Sub
```

This is a quick fix used when a redesign forces the issue. Don't make it a habit. Again, common routines and variables should be written in BAS files that can be shared between forms.

I Do Declare

You can declare multiple variables on one line by separating them with commas. There's just one little thing to remember. Pass this short quiz and you can declare with the best of them.

I am trying to define four local string variables. Which of the following statements fails to do this?

1. Dim ls_one As String, ls_two As String, ls_three As String, ls_four As String
2. Dim ls_one$, ls_two$, ls_three$, ls_four$
3. Dim ls_one, ls_two, ls_three, ls_four As String

The answer: 3. Only **ls_four** is declared as a string. The other three variables will be type variant.

You can separate variables with commas, but unlike some other languages, you can't use one *As type* statement to define them all. The code will probably run anyway since the variant type is happy to take on any assignment but it's operating with a false assumption. Later on I might try to pass **ls_one** as a variable to a function that declared this argument as a string. The result will be a "Parameter type mismatch" error. If I failed the quiz, I'll have no idea why. I learned this lesson the hard way during my first week of VB programming.

The Show Waits for No One

Just keep one thing straight with the **Show** command: If you issue the regular modeless **Show** command, the calling procedure doesn't wait around for the newly shown form to get unloaded or hidden to finish processing. It keeps on going. If you issue the modal **Show** command, the calling procedure does wait for the newly shown form to get unloaded or hidden to finish processing. It'll hang around all day. If you forget this, your show might bring down the house.

Example: I want to display a popup form. The user enters a value into the text box on this popup form then presses a command button that hides the form. I then want to assign the value entered in this text box to a local variable.

This calling procedure doesn't do what I hoped for:

```
Dim ls_name As String

frm_popup.Show    'Doesn't wait for an answer from frm_popup

ls_name = frm_popup.txt_name.Text 'Won't work
```

This does:

```
Dim ls_name As String

frm_popup.Show MODAL  'Sticks here like glue until frm_popup is
    ⇨hidden or unloaded

ls_name = frm_popup.txt_name.Text        'Gets the entered value
```

Here's a somewhat subtle technique using the **Show** command. A **Show** can be issued in the **load** event of a non-modal form. If the form load takes a long time because of complicated processing, the **Show** command can be issued before any heavy coding. This way users have something to look at besides an hourglass prompt while they're waiting. It might encourage them to stick around a little longer before they reboot the machine. One other advantage to using **Show** here is that, normally, you can't set focus to a control in the **load** event of a form. If you do an explicit **SetFocus** command an "Illegal function call" message will result. Issuing a **Show** command before the **SetFocus** will solve this problem.

```
Sub Form_Load

    Show
```

```
            txt_name.SetFocus       'O.K. since I did a Show
End Sub
```

This might prove useful if the form load calls a subroutine to clear and reset controls and variables. This routine might clear all the data controls, reset flags, initialize variables, and set focus to the first control in the tab order. Say you want to call this routine in various places—at the form load, clear command button, after the save of data, and so on. That would be good, one common form-level routine to simplify and centralize processing. This is what I live for. Alas, such a beauty, but I can't call you from the form load with your pesky little SetFocus hanging around. Just when all hope is lost, good old Show steps in to save the code and the relationship. (I know, I know, I've got to get out more.)

The Three Trues

The following properties must be set to True (or False) depending on your intentions:

> Form level: **KeyPreview = True** (False is default):
> This is necessary if you want to trap keystrokes at the form level, otherwise the form's **KeyPress**, **KeyDown**, and **KeyUp** events won't get triggered. If you forget to do this, then any code placed in these form-level events won't get executed no matter how hard you slam down the keys.
> Form level: **AutoRedraw = True** (False is default):
> This is necessary if you are drawing graphics on the screen and don't want them erased after being hidden when the current form is resized or overlaid by another window. A call to a popup form might otherwise wipe your picture clean. I used this once when drawing grid lines on a WYSIWYG form designer.
> VB Grid control: **HighLight = True** (True is default):
> The selected cells in the grid will be highlighted. Useful for emphasizing the current row being edited. Otherwise, it's difficult to determine the selected row.

The following code highlights the entire grid row just clicked if the **Highlight = True**:

```
Sub Grd_Data_Click ()

    'Select clicked row as current row
```

```
                           grd_data.SelStartCol = 1
                           grd_data.SelEndCol = grd_data.Cols - 1

                           'Highlight row
                           grd_data.SelStartRow = grd_data.Row
                           grd_data.SelEndRow = grd_data.Row
             End Sub
```

You know by now that I don't waste my time writing generic processes like the previous example at the control level. Practice your global writing skills and convert that code into a generic routine that is called using a grid as an argument variable.

Arrays

Unless you declare **Option Base 1**, you can begin your arrays with subscript 0. Thus, a fixed array actually gives you one more than the subscript declared.

```
       Static ls_array(4) As String

       ls_array(0) = "I"
       ls_array(1) = "Hate"
       ls_array(2) = "Array"
       ls_array(3) = "Element"
       ls_array(4) = "Zero"
```

I'm no he-man C monster. I hate using the 0 subscript. As a maintenance programmer, when I find that someone has started assignments to the 0 subscript for processes that themselves don't begin with it 0, I want to heave.

Look at this **i = (i-1)** junk.

```
       grd_data.Col = 1
       For i = 1 to grd_data.Rows
             grd_data.Row = i
             grd_data.Text = fs_array(i-1)
       Next i
```

This loon has decided to use a 0-based array to store and reset grid data that begins with row 1. Every assignment has to remember this and work a step behind. The code is dragging its leg. Here, it's not so bad, but when I'm snaking around a big project maintaining code, I don't want to remember that Ol' Jethro decided to use the 0 element. For maintenance sake, don't mismatch subscripts. I've never put anything in the 0 subscript. The world doesn't start counting at 0. "Three dollars change, sir: Here you go, 0, 1, 2, 3 dollars." That store's not staying in business very long.

I prefer dynamic arrays over static arrays. I live vicariously through their brazen flexibility. Dynamic arrays can be set to a different sizes depending on the circumstances using the **ReDim** statement. The neat thing is that a dynamic array initially set to a particular size with a **ReDim** statement with data already assigned to its elements can still add other subscripts without losing the current data. A standard ReDim statement will flush out any values currently in the array. By using the **ReDim Preserve** statement, the original data is saved.

Here's a useless example that shows off dynamic array processing in all its glory.

```
Dim li_ctr As Integer

Static ls_array() As String

ReDim ls_array(3)

ls_array(1) = "Dynamic"

ls_array(2) = "Arrays"

ls_array(3) = "Are"

For li_ctr = 1 To UBound(ls_array)

      MsgBox (ls_array(li_ctr))

Next li_ctr


'I love the next statement

ReDim Preserve ls_array(UBound(ls_array) + 1)      'Add one more
      ⇨subscript, but save data. Wow.

ls_array(UBound(ls_array)) = "Cool"      'Assign value to new
      ⇨subscript element. Also wow.


For li_ctr = 1 to UBound(ls_array)

      MsgBox(ls_array(li_ctr))

Next li_ctr
```

One strange problem with dynamic arrays is that even when using **Option Explicit,** the compiler doesn't pick up a misspelled array name in a **ReDim** statement. It's then possible to issue a **ReDim** statement to an array that doesn't exist. Later on, a "Subscript out of range" error will result since the actual array wasn't redimensionalized. Be careful with this. A mysterious out of range error might be from a typo.

Example:

```
Static ls_array() As String

ReDim ls_aray(5)        'Misspelled ls_array

ls_array(1) = "a"       'Subscript out of range' error will result
```

Dynamic and elusive. They're just so damn cool.

Hidden Treasures or Ignorant Developer?

Everlasting Variables

Form-level variables maintain their values even when the form is unloaded. This is not consistent with the form's objects, which will clear out and reset any properties set dynamically when unloaded. Therefore, remember to clear or reset any variables in the **Load** or **Activate** event that shouldn't maintain their old values. I wasted a whole morning learning this one the hard way. There's a sentence on this in the VB manual. (It should've been in a 100-point font.)

Double Duty String

In addition to being used to declare a character type variable, the keyword **String** is also a VB function. It returns a string filled with a single character. It's easy to overlook or forget this; I keep thinking the function is called **Fill** or something and can never find it. If you're as dumb as I am, here's an example of the elusive command.

```
Dim ls_line As String
ls_line = String(100, "_")
```

Equivalent statement using the ANSI code instead:

```
ls_line = String(100, 95)
```

The variable **ls_line** is now a hundred little underscores. A statement using this command is a lot easier to write and maintain than one that assigns a variable to a long string of characters.

Shift-Tab

VB does a good job with block selection processing. You can select a block of code, then copy, delete, paste, and more. You can also select a whole section of code, then press the **Tab** key and indent it all en masse. This is very useful in nested logic when you want to indent long subprocesses. I figured that out pretty quickly, but it took me a long time before I realized you could pull the whole block back again using **Shift-Tab**. I'd drag them back over line by line. Don't follow my lead.

Combo Box Style = 2: I'll Never Change

If you use a combo box with the Style property set to 2 - Dropdown List, then don't put code in the **change** event because it doesn't get triggered. You can select different items all day long, but the code will just sit there and shrug. You must move any code you want to put in the **change** event into the **click** event. I'm maintaining a program right now that had this problem in it. For three years, the code has been sitting idle in this nontriggered event. I'm glad it wasn't me who put it there.

InStr

Don't settle for a poor imitation. **Instr** returns the first occurrence of one string within another. Some people don't realize there's an **InStr** function, and they step though using a for loop and look at each character using the **mid$** command. Why write it if VB does it for you?

Behold the **InStr** function:

```
li_position = InStr(ls_text, "X")
```

Much better than:

```
For li_ctr = 1 to Len(ls_text)
    If Mid$(ls_text,li_ctr,1) = "X" Then
        li_position = li_ctr
        Exit For
```

```
        End If
    Next li_ctr
```

Exit Do, Exit For: Enough Already

Here's a more serious inefficiency I see occasionally in do and for loops. The desired item is found but the logic just keeps on going, checking all the rest of the values. After you find what you're looking for, get the heck out of there using the appropriate **Exit** statement.

```
    ll_ctr = 1
    Do While ll_ctr < 10000000
        If fi_array(ll_ctr) = -9999 Then
            ll_item = ll_ctr
        End If
        ll_ctr = ll_ctr + 1
    Loop
```

The element **fi_array(1)** might equal -9999 and trigger the assignment to **li_item**, but this loop will keep running until all 10,000,000 elements are processed. An **Exit** Do should be put after the assignment unless your logic is searching for the last item of a multiple set.

```
    ll_ctr = 1
    Do While ll_ctr < 10000000
        If fi_array(ll_ctr) = -9999 Then
            ll_item = ll_ctr
            Exit Do 'Much Better
        End If
        ll_ctr = ll_ctr + 1
    Loop
```

(Yeah, I know; you can't have an array with 10 million elements in it. I'm trying to scare the wannabes, all right?)

Syntax Checking

I love **Option Explicit** more than anyone, but I can't stand VB's default line-by-line syntax checking. Every time you hit **Enter**, the nosy little thing sees what your up to and starts balking. I'd rather save these announcements for later on when I'm actually going to run the project. You can stop this incessant syntax checking by

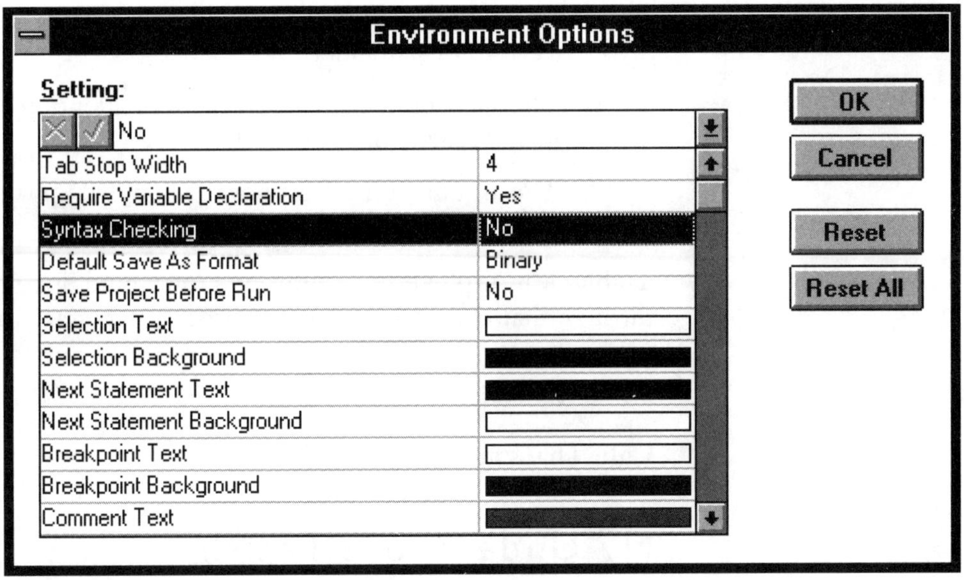

FIGURE 5.6 Syntax checking environment option.

selecting the menu item Options—Environment—Syntax Checking = No (Figure 5.6). It's right next to good old **Option Explicit**.

My Strange Obsessions

You want anal-retentive? You got anal-retentive. Here's a few more coding standards I adhere to because I'm just strange and obsessive. I also think the code is easier to read and maintain using these standards. If you want clearer code (or are just strange and obsessive), you might consider giving them a try.

Why Don't You Ever Call?

Let's further refine the process of calling a subroutine. It is not a VB requirement that you use the keyword **Call** before subroutine call, but it makes the code immeasurably easy to scan read.

Example:

```
Call sb_Sort_Recs(100, 200)
```

I like that statement. It's looks like a subroutine call. Using the keyword **Call** leaves no doubt about it:

☆ **Call** switches to the VB color for keywords. It stands out in a crowd of statements.

☆ The subroutine name itself snaps to attention behind it, forced exactly one step back.

☆ The argument list must now be bundled up with parentheses, not left out swaying in white space.

Tight, clear, explicit. No confusion. Your mind doesn't need go through that two-second compile process necessary to get a bearing on:

```
Sort_Recs 100, 200
```

Ugh. That statement just makes me sick.

My Underscore Fetish

I guess you've noticed that I use underscores in all my variable, routine, and control names. I like to separate the descriptive name from the data type (li_ctr, fs_EMP_NAME, gs_database). Also, whenever I see anything with an underscore in it, I know it's one of my own creations. None of VB's commands, functions, or properties include an underscore character. Once again, I want to save that two-second compile process when scrolling though a routine. (Am I lazy or what?)

Naked Rear Ends

Most programs I've seen do a good job indenting subprocesses within nested for-next or if-then statements:

```
For li_row = 1 to 10
    For li_col = 1 to 10
        For li_char = 1 to 10
            'Million lines of code
        Next
    Next
Next

If (li_row = 1) And (li_col = 1) and (li_flag = "Y") Then
    If li_status = "P" Then
        'Million lines of code
    End If
End If
```

The indenting is good. What I don't like is those buck-naked **End If** and **Next** statements. I often see code without the counter variable included in the **Next** statement. VB lets you get away with it. This is okay for processing that fits easily on a single screen. If the code is indented properly, you scan up to find **Next**'s companion **For** statement. Once your code spreads out over multiple pages, all you see is the skinny little legs dangling from the top of your screen:

```
                    'Million lines of code

          Next

      Next

  Next
```

Next what? You have to scroll all around to figure out which next statement belongs to which for statement. I suggest you always explicitly use the counter variable in the for loop.

Here the next statements are dressed for the occasion:

```
                    'Million lines of code

          Next li_char

      Next li_col

  Next li_row
```

Far more tasteful.

I insist on the same propriety for **End If** statements. This requires adding a little comment statement to cover the bare limbs.

```
                    'Million lines of code

      End If    '(li_row = 1) And (li_col = 1) and (li_flag = "Y")

  End If    'li_status = "P"
```

Now I know what's going on in there without having to snoop around. I add the same obsessive little comment in **Select Case** statements:

```
      End Select 'Case li_ctr
```

These little fineries make debugging easier. A forgotten **End If**, **Next**, or **Select Case** statement within a tangle of code can take a long time to find. I also hate scrolling around to figure out what should be obvious. Putting a little comment after an **End If** statement is the only thing I learned in my one computer course in college. The programs were written in Pascal so we used French braces. Fifteen weeks, and all I got out of it was {}.

API Calls : The Ridiculous and the Sublime

One book your development group should probably consider purchasing is a comprehensive API manual. It will list the API calls available to VB and how and when to use them. Unfortunately, these books are exhaustive, and you've got to muck through hundreds of API calls that are listed alphabetically. The useful and vital APIs are lined up rank and file with those that are ridiculous or absurd. To help focus your search through the manual in the following sections, I've listed the API calls that have either been specifically referenced in preceding chapter sections or are useful in supporting the ideas.

You really don't need a lot of API calls to do development work, but in some cases they are your best or only option. Since setting up an API call is usually tedious and mechanical, I suggest (as I always do) to convert any code examples in the book to global routines placed in one or more API-specific BAS files as explained in "Chapter 2, The Global Arena." Any API book will fully explain the full parameter setup and calling process necessary to use the following calls.

Chapter 2, The Global Variable: Pathway to Exotic Data Locales

Reading private INI files:
GetPrivateProfileString
Writing to private INI files:
WritePrivateProfileString
Reading WIN.INI files:
GetProfileString
Writing to WIN.INI:
WriteProfileString

An INI or initialization file is a standard ASCII text file. All INI files, WIN.INI and private files alike, are set up the same way.

Here's a small piece of my own WIN.INI file:
[Cardfile]
ValidateFileWrite=1

[Paintbrush]
OmitPictureFormat=0

```
width=799
height=560
clear=COLOR
```

An INI file is broken into sections. Each section is denoted by a header encased in brackets. Here, **Cardfile** and **Paintbrush** are the entombed section headings. Within a section, there are one or more variable names and the value that's returned for this variable when reading the INI file. I might write an API call that says, "Give me the value for height in the [Paintbrush] section of WIN.INI," and it would return 560. Of course, in your application, it's more likely you'll say something like, "Give me the value for database in the [Data] section of APP.INI." That certainly seems more useful. But just think, now I know my Paintbrush height is 560. I would have sworn it was at least 575.

Try not to write anything application-specific to the WIN.INI file. It's already filled with enough junk from every other Windows application. Most likely, your application-specific INI file will reside on the network in the directory that also contains the EXE(s) files. Whatever you do, just don't use that awful hard-code for your data path.

Chapter 2, Overall Application Setup: Dodge City

Executing another VB program from your application:
  WinExec

This is used if you are launching separate sub-EXEs from a master EXE. You can run these programs with either the **Shell** command or the **WinExec** API call. The only advantage to **WinExec** is that it returns an error code you can check, so you can put up a more graceful error message then the standard VB harangue.

Chapter 3, Windows Training: One Click Makes You Smaller

Preventing multiple copies of an application from being loaded:
  GetModuleHandle
  GetModuleUsage

I've mentioned that users who lose sight of a currently running application by accidentally clicking the workspace tend to just load the whole thing all over again. If your application shouldn't allow multiple copies to be running all at once, then use these API calls. If you decide you need to do this, I'd also suggest you include a rather verbose message box that gives the user some clue as to how to find the currently running application either by using **Alt-Tab** or **Ctrl-Esc** (Figure 5.7). Otherwise, I guarantee frantic calls to the help desk.

Chapter 3, Dress Blue: The Template Form

Modifying a form's control menu:
   GetSystemMenu
   ModifyMenu
   DeleteMenu

I know that having a control box is standard in most Windows applications. I also know that new users can get tied up in knots if they get trapped in its clutches. If you've decided to eliminate the control box from all VB forms as standard development practice, you'll need these APIs to handle MDI parents. The rest of the forms come along quietly by assigning the property **ControlBox = False**.

Chapter 5, Data-Caching Techniques

Changing the TabStop in a list box:
   SendMessage
   GetDialogBaseUnits
   GetFocus

These API calls are used to set a tab stop wider than the display width of the list box. Then one or more data fields can be hidden

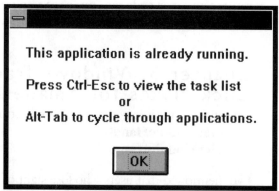

FIGURE 5.7 Application already running message.

from view. This is quite a little dance. If you prefer to sit in the bleachers, then use a multitude of spaces to hide the fields from view.

Chapter 6, Oh, DLL, DLL! Wherefore Art Thou DLL ?

Check for the existence of DLLs and other files:

GetWindowsDirectory
GetSystemDirectory

I've mentioned that some special DLLs might be required, depending on your application. To make sure that certain files are located in a user's Windows or Windows system directory, use these API calls in conjunction with a global function that checks for the existence of a file.

These API calls return the user's Windows and Windows system directory. There's no guarantee that Windows was installed in C:\WINDOWS\, so don't erroneously make this assumption in your applications. First, get the location of the Windows or Windows system directory, then check for the desired file. If it doesn't exist, then put up a hysterical warning message including the name and location of the file and who to call for help. Putting this little trap in once saved me a day's work (based on having wasted a whole day before I added the trap).

Using the global functions I set up in "The Mighty BAS" in Chapter 2, the trap would look something like this:

```
Dim ls_file_name As String

ls_file_name = gfn_get_dir("SYSTEM") + "\MSAFINX.DLL"

If gfn_FileExists(ls_file_name) = False Then

    MsgBox("The file " + ls_file_name + " is missing." + Chr(13)
        ⇨+ Chr(10) + "Contact the help desk.")

    End

End If
```

Much better than a mysterious crash later on in the application.

Chapter 6, Windows Troubleshooting Triptych

Determining the amount of Windows resources available:

GetFreeSystemResources

If you have a program that consistently crashes when system resources fall below a certain level, you can use this API call to warn users of the impending doom. Hopefully, this will encourage them to exit and reenter Windows to refresh resources, or just unload the seven copies of Space Monkeys they have running.

Not Referenced in Any Chapter, but I Used It Once Anyway

Exit Windows entirely

ExitWindows

This API call will exit Windows when called from your application. You might be running an overnight batch or download program and want to exit Windows when the process is complete. Possibly an application error might be so severe that it warrants throwing the user out of Windows. In either case, this API call will return the machine back to the savage DOS land.

CHAPTER *six*

TROUBLESHOOTING

Besides hunkering down and writing code, programmers often need to troubleshoot problems related to an application or computers in general. This can be a fun change of pace or a painful waste of time depending on the situation, your personality, and the parties involved. The following sections cover some common troubleshooting situations I've encountered.

Windows Troubleshooting Triptych

If you start getting erratic behavior while programming in VB, or your executables suddenly start crashing, try the following:

1. Check your Windows System Resources (Figure 6.1). If it's low, that could be the problem right there. Windows isn't always able to reallocate resources, so as different software is loaded and unloaded it slowly shrivels away. My tell-tale sign of low resources is when a form's fancy fonts degrade to Courier. Unexpected VB "Out of Memory" error messages may appear in your project once you go below a certain resource level. Exit Windows to rejuvenate.

2. Now that you're back in DOS land, you can try the following: Check your WINDOWS\TEMP directory. If there are any files there, then delete them. Don't do this while you're running Windows since they might be in use. Anything still in there after exiting Windows is a temporary file left from an application that crashed. I don't know if these files do any harm but they do take up space.

3. Run the DOS command **CHKDSK /F**. Turn the lost clusters into files, then delete the files. I know this seems weird, but I've seen this fix bizarre problems three times already.

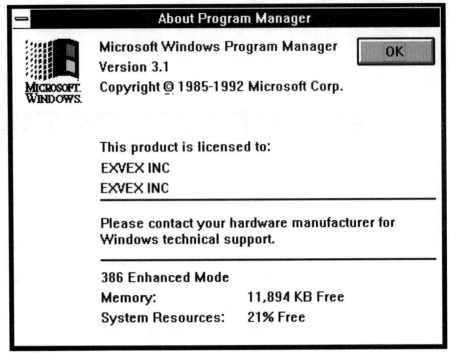

FIGURE 6.1 No wonder it's not working.

Again, don't do this while you're in Windows (it won't let you even if you try). Consider adding these lines to your AUTOEXEC.BAT:

```
DEL C:\WINDOWS\TEMP\*.*
CHKDSK /F
```

Printing Troubles

Here's the one Windows printing problem that I've run into several times. It happened on a user's computer just after I finished this chapter. It's very simple, but if you don't check for it first, you'll do all kinds of unnecessary things. Go into the Control Panel and load the Printers option. Check the default printer (Figure 6.2). If it says "No Default Printer," then nothing's going to print. A computer will sometimes lose its default, to the dismay of the user. Just set the appropriate default printer from the list. In the worst case, there's no list to begin with and you'll have to go find the Windows installation diskettes and add one.

One of the most common printing problem on a Novell network is having the timeout set too low. Large and graphics-intensive documents need time to get ready before the job is queued to the printer, otherwise a very weird-looking document can come out. Check the user's current print setup by typing **CAPTURE /SHOW**, and look for the Timeout Count. You may have to increase the **ti = *number*** section of the capture command to get certain print jobs to come out properly.

```
C:\>capture s=it/q=it_laser/ff/nt/nb/ti=2


C:\>CAPTURE /SHOW

LPT1: Capturing data to server IT queue IT_LASER.

       User will not be notified after the files are printed.

             Capture Defaults:Disabled Automatic Endcap:Enabled

             Banner :(None) Form Feed :Yes

             Copies :1 Tabs :No conversion

             Form :0 Timeout Count :2 seconds
```

Maybe two seconds isn't enough time. Let's up it and try the print job again.

```
C:\>capture s=it/q=it_laser/ff/nt/nb/ti=30
```

When troubleshooting, try to isolate whether this is a printing problem or a network printing problem. See if the problem occurs when using a printer directly connected to the computer, bypassing all the network stuff. This can involve lugging a printer to a user's desk, so save this for late in the process. If it's a network problem,

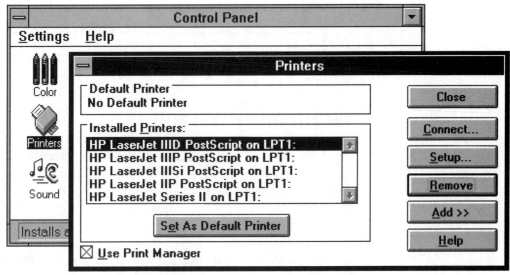

FIGURE 6.2 No default, no printout.

then you might be able to pass the troubleshooting burden over to the CNEs.

Here's my favorite problem. You cannot print to a network printer if you are not logged on to the network. Sometimes users have software on their local hard drives and they try to print. They forgot to log on and then get weird error messages. I've seen some wild explanations offered when this was the real problem. Check this first, before you go off and recable the network. Otherwise you'll never live it down.

Sacrificing A Virgin

One benefit of being a software developer is that your computer is chock full of good stuff. DLLs and VBXs and device drivers are installed separately then forgotten. There you sit, a jaded old dragon, languishing on a pile of gold. Once you decide to share your application with the peasants, you'll find that not all are blessed with such treasures.

Installing a Windows application was summarized perfectly by our hardware/network specialist. "It's a sloppy mess." Depending on the status of the user's computer before the install, a whole kingdom of files needs to be included. The list could include Windows itself, device drivers, special files to allow access to the SQL server, DLLs, VBXs, and updates to certain files like WIN.INI. The user probably also needs an additional mapping to the network drive and directory that contains your application's executable files. This must all be tested, and everything must work together on a computer that nobody's ever seen before. It's probably easier to rent time on your own development PC.

Nothing is going to make this process easy. One helpful addition to the installation procedure is a "virgin PC." (Everyone relishes saying "virgin PC"; the reason still escapes me.) The search for a suitable candidate may turn up an old 386 with 4 megs of memory. You want the saddest computer that might currently be in use in the organization. This PC is then wiped clean, its hard drive is reformatted, and it's checked for viruses. It's stripped all the way down to COMMAND.COM. On top of this is installed the barest configuration a user's computer might have, probably just Windows and the standard directories and files needed to log in to the network. If possible, keep this bare bones configuration saved somewhere on the network so the computer can easily be wiped clean and the files copied down for each new test of an install procedure.

Using this computer, run through the entire procedure that will be used to install your application on users' PCs. Find out any problems here, before you run off to the far reaches of Userland and get mysterious "Property Not Found" error messages. The whole install procedure, start to finish, should be written down. Create install diskettes containing all the necessary files, including a text file of the setup procedure you just diligently recorded.

Oh DLL, DLL! Wherefore Art Thou DLL?

VB's financial functions require a special DLL to run. I now know that the **DateAdd** function requires the **MSAFINX.DLL** to be in the WINDOWS\SYSTEM directory. I wish I knew that when the application was continuously crashing on users' machines. If you are getting mysterious crashes on some machines, do a DLL check. Check if any DLLs are missing or are a different version than on other machines. Run this check on INI files and VBXs as well. There is a list in the back of the VB manual of the DLLs that might be required by the application. Make sure these are included in the installation.

Applications on a Network: Stand Up for Your Rights

In a networked application it's important to check the rights of the users. Most programmers are granted full rights to the development area when working so they can copy and delete files, and so on. However, users may be running with a considerably more limited Rights Mask. Always run a test of the application with the rights of a typical user. I lost a day and a half and a fistful of hair on this one. If possible, have a dummy user account set up on the network for such purposes.

The same rights testing also applies to the SQL server. If you're developing applications and logging in as SA or some other superuser account, then you have rights to do just about anything. The hapless users who aren't running in this God mode might be unable to perform certain operations. Don't design a program that runs only with rights the users won't be granted. I did. Big dummy.

Upgrades: Progress Is a Comfortable Disease

Any upgrade, whether it's to Visual Basic, a third-party VBX , the SQL server, DOS, the network, or whatever, should be approached cautiously. We upgraded a single developer's computer to the new version of a database add-on, and the SQL calls in the VB applications ran about five times slower than before. Remember, you are often acting as a beta site with some of these products. This means you are effectively doing the testing of the product for the company that has rushed it out to meet a release date.

Usually, there is no going back when upgrading Windows software. The install process dumps new versions of DLLs, VBXs, and other stuff into the \WINDOWS\SYSTEM directory, overwriting without confirmation any old version. You don't realize what you've missed until its gone. Once converted, you're stuck. First back up the computer before installing a new version of anything. We needed to restore the entire drive when we wanted to back out of that disastrous database add-on upgrade. Upgrades to the SQL server may nullify some of your old working SQL calls. Cautiously create test databases (using those SQL scripts discussed in the section "Play It Again Sam") and run through the application.

Why should you upgrade? After all, if it's working, why mess with it?

The obvious reason is that the upgrade is just what it says it is: an improvement over the old version with new features, bug fixes, and all that rot. The hidden reason is you might lose technical support. Vendors don't necessarily support older versions of their software. Other products, especially newer releases, might be compatible only with the latest version.

Whatever you do, don't get ambitious and upgrade your server, DOS, VB, and everything else all at once. There's no way anything will ever work again. One thing at a time. Test, rinse, repeat, then move on to the next upgrade.

Back Up: You're Just Not My Type

Make sure you make personal backups of all current work. Do this even if your files are on a network that is backed up daily. However the source files are stored, store the backups in some other type of media. If the files are on the network, don't just copy them to another network directory. Put them on your local hard drive. Back up local files to the network or floppies. Make a quick copy of your program to a hold area if you are going to make drastic changes. You may find out the old way was the right way.

Backing up your application's program files is vital. Even more critical is backing up the data, whether it's in a SQL database or flat files. The most important part of the backup process is the restore. If you can't retrieve the file after you back it up, then the whole thing isn't much use. Don't assume that because you saved your files or database you'll get the information back. We discovered that a month of tape backups of our SQL server didn't really work. The data couldn't be restored. Test whatever process you are using to back up data. If you rely on your company's network administrators for backup, call and request that a certain file or directory be restored. See how they handle this task. It's best to find out how reliable their backup procedure is before you really need it.

It's probably overkill to back up your own computer every day if your applications are developed on a network drive. You should, however, have at least one full backup of your computer once the complete suite of development tools are installed: Windows, Visual Basic, any add-on products, the network device drivers, and so on. This way, if your computer gets fried for whatever reason, you don't have to run around reinstalling all the necessary software and returning everything to the way you like it.

While backing up is necessary, it's important to know when to let go. I've seen six old versions of an application nestled together in subdirectories under the most current version. If you really need every old release of a system for administrative or nostalgic purposes, then save it to tape. Don't clog up the development environment with megs of ancient code. You don't want someone to end up writing a lot of new code and suddenly realize he or she is working in a system that's two generations old.

The Demo: Die with Your Boots On

When I first started out my computer career as a grunt tester, one of my responsibilities was setting up for the system demos with the users. All the effort you put into creating a professional application can go down the drain if you screw up getting the demo ready. They used to tell me 15 minutes beforehand, and it used to drive me crazy. There is no worse first impression to clients or users than watching the development crew run around trying to jump-start a stalled application. Everyone's muttering incantations about device drivers and config files with a look of stone-cold fear in their eyes. Then you end up resorting to transparencies with an overhead projector instead of showing the actual system.

Before any meeting where the actual system will be demonstrated make sure the application runs—not on a computer, not on your computer, but on *the computer in the meeting room*. Check the day before, then again at least one hour before the demo.

Quick checklist for the meeting room:
1. Do you have the computer, a network connection, a good mouse, a mouse pad?
2. How is the keyboard? Is it different from what the demonstrator normally uses? Will that affect anything?
3. Has the room and any necessary equipment been reserved? Are you really, really sure about this? If an executive board meeting has been scheduled at the same time, they will throw you out in the hall.

Make sure everyone in the development group knows about the demo and that nobody tries to do something wild while it's going on. This is not the time to run a system backup or update your executables or in any way manage to shove your hands into the demo's whirling blades.

If the demo is a road show, then the possibility of something going wrong will increase enormously. One salesman came to our site to demo a database add-on and forgot to bring the computer he always used. The one he had didn't have the system installed properly, and nothing worked. All he could do was offer the feeble, "Well, it runs on my other computer." No sale that day. I saw a report generator demo during which the program crashed every time it ran because there was no printer attached. No sale that day either.

To minimize such catastrophes, make sure you call ahead and find out what you're up against. Find out what equipment they have, what you need to bring, and everything else from the quick checklist. Give the person presenting the demo complete written instructions for setting up the hardware and running the application. I went so far as to put labels on the ends of the cables so they would know where they went (yes, this was necessary). Make whoever will be assigned the setup task do a dry run in-house before venturing out. It is not enough that you can do it. That person should be able to do the entire setup, with no help or prompting, preferably blindfolded while standing on one foot. Remember, with a road show demo, there won't be a gaggle of techies scurrying around to help your salesperson out.

No matter where you have the demo, make sure that if you bring up any data it won't prove embarrassing. You want to minimize the impression that the application is being developed by juvenile delinquents (which is most likely the situation; visit my office for confirmation). It's best to create a database used only for demos and fill it with sensible data: no users named Jock Strap or Big Butt, profane login passwords, endless comment fields all filled with "QOIUWQY-WUIYQYTEYQYQW" or passionate odes to Kristara Barrington.

Troubleshooting Summary: The Whole World Changes

The previous sections were just a small sampling of the problems that can arise during development. I don't wish to drone on about every stupid thing that's ever happened to me. I'll stop with the specifics now and try a little general theory.

Let me summarize what I've learned about programming, computers, and troubleshooting in the last four years. Once you understand this, your experiences will make more sense. It's grim, but so am I.

1. Nothing ever works.
2. When it works, it's waiting not to work.

The first question to ask when someone comes to you with a problem is, "Did it ever work?" If so, then the second question (which they won't be able to answer) is, "What has happened since then?" Something has indeed happened, and I've seen that it can be just about anything—a crimped network cable, a downed T1 line, a missing DLL, the monitor isn't plugged in, or the floppy disk was put in the drive the wrong way. I've also come to realize that the likelihood of anything happening, no matter how ridiculous, is 50 percent.

When troubleshooting, make no assumptions and change only one thing at a time. Begin by examining the simplest cause of the problem. Start with most labor-free fix possible. Work your way up to the more complicated and absurd causes and solutions. I mention this because some people get this process backward and start tearing the walls apart unnecessarily. Drastic measures might need to be taken, but only after the simpler options have been explored.

Unfortunately, the only way to get good at troubleshooting is to suffer. You must experience, then store away, all the wretched problems you've encountered. When a new problem arises, you must stop, turn to stone, ignore the lamentations of the people around you, and revisit every nightmare you've ever been through, and see how it applies to the current situation.

I've found that troubleshooting works best with two people. One should be calm and rational to filter the ideas. The other should ramble on, uninhibited, suggesting every hare-brained scheme he or she can imagine. I used to be the ranter. After we tried the obvious solutions, I'd just spout out every horrible thing that ever happened to me. The other guy would throw out 99 percent of what I said. Eventually, I'd make some sense.

When I was still attending computer school, I met a man on a PATH train. He mentioned he was a paranoid-schizophrenic, and after a short conversation I had little reason to doubt him. He told me something that you should understand if you are going to be a successful programmer or troubleshooter. I think about it every day. He held out his hand, palm down, and looked at me.

> *"When I go like this,"* he then bent his finger slightly,
> *barely enough to notice, "the whole world changes."*

No matter what you do, no matter how small or insignificant, after you're finished, the whole world changes.

Every
      single
           time.

Here's my favorite troubleshooting example. An executive in our company was given a fancy new mouse for her computer. She called the help desk complaining that the mouse would stop working at 10:00 A.M. and wouldn't work for the rest of the morning. Upon returning from lunch the mouse worked fine. This would happen every day. What was the problem? She was given one of those fancy new mice that used a photo diode. The bright morning sun flooded her office, rendering the sensor inoperable. As morning changed to midday, the sun passed and all was well again.

> *The sun heralds in*
> *the start of a new day,*
> *and the*
> *whole*
> *world*
> *changes.*

THE LIFE AND TIMES OF AN IN-HOUSE APPLICATION

There's a big difference between writing VB programs at home and developing an actual application that will be used in your company. When developing a corporate application, a programmer will often be at the mercy of many other individuals who can, depending on their ability or temperament, make things unbearable. A lot of people can be involved in the development process: project leaders, systems analysts, junior and senior programmers, testers, technical writers, business analysts, and of course the beloved user community. The following sections touch on some of the personal aspects of development as well as the life and times of in-house applications.

The User Meeting

For the most part, I am tucked away in a private office far away from any contact with human beings. I come in, stare at a screen for about eight hours, then leave. Everyone in the company feels more comfortable knowing people like me aren't running around loose in the building. The user meeting is one of the controlled situations during which they unlock my cage and allow me to mix with the general population. As a programmer developing in-house applications, you will inevitably be required to attend such meetings. The purpose of the meeting will vary. Possibly it's an application demo, spec analysis, or a "We hate this lousy system" forum. Meetings with users are always traumatic. The technical problems are covered in the previous section "The Demo: Die with Your Boots On." This section is more about what to expect from the users than from the hardware. Your experiences will vary slightly but will follow the same themes.

The one basic tenet to remember in any business meeting is that, after the first hour, nobody is paying attention any more. The best time to schedule a meeting is probably 10:00 A.M. After two hours, there's a reason to break for lunch. Nobody is really awake enough to participate in a 9:00 A.M. meeting, and most of the discussion will revolve around obtaining coffee and buttered rolls. Late in the day, everyone is itching to get home already. People will be shifting in their seats like first graders with weak bladders. Any topic will be agreed to at 5:15 P.M., but this is justly considered coercion.

Never, ever expect users to be impressed with what you have done. It's hard not to get excited about the program you just did that seems like it's just what everyone was begging for. One minute into the demo and everyone's ripping it apart, often attacking the feature that was just requested a week ago. This is not a glorious career. No one cares when it works, only when it breaks. The most you can hope for in any demo is stunned silence. Also remember the following eternal user conditions:

> No one will care about the new feature you just killed yourself over, even though last week they said it was vital beyond words.
> Nobody remembers asking for the features you put in.
>> Everyone remembers the feature you forgot.
> New users will want everything done differently.

If you put some useless doodad in the program just as a freebie, like pulling up the Windows Calculator, the users will become transfixed with it. Nothing will be able to divert their attention from it. Can it export to SAS? Can we add an OCR interface to read my lab data? This usually happens when showing a real feature that you thought everyone was going to fawn over. Menu items for processes that don't exist yet are also great user lures. There's no code behind them, they don't do anything, yet they can sidetrack an entire meeting.

If an in-house application is shown to executives, they will immediately want to sell it on the market for a million dollars. The system might only save names and addresses to a flat file, but they'll call up Microsoft and try to get a merger going.

You will finally get to meet other people in the organization through these meetings. Try as they might, the rest of the members of the organization can't help but think of a meeting with the development group as a trip to the Freak Show. Their minds are already made up and there's no possibility of convincing them that you're a group of well-adjusted, socially facile individuals who pursue a wide variety of interests and activities. Don't even try. Eventually one of these users will be a woman so unspeakably beautiful that all men in the development group will become smitten. She will have a luminous arc of hair, kind eyes and a gentle smile. Her skin will be clear and smooth, not made up of tiny pixels like a GIF file. You will speak her name softly, as if a prayer. Bizarre images will leap to mind, perhaps of barefoot pilgrims prostrating a journey of a thousand miles just to gaze at her image, cast in bronze, stored in a temple constructed for this sole purpose. She will, of course, turn out to be one of the most demanding and annoying users anyone has ever dealt with, and down comes the shrine.

You will demo an application to the same user group several times, making any necessary changes along the way. In the third or fourth user meeting, someone will suddenly notice a field, feature, or process that has been there since the very beginning. This person (probably a manager) will become seized with rage and demand an explanation for the offending item. The head will shake from side to side and he or she will grip the arms of the chair. "That invalidates everything! This system is totally useless!" I've seen otherwise rational people go into this beserker-mode. I'm still puzzled about the reason behind it. Usually the fix is quite minor, and your project leader should be able to calm the person down.

Outbursts occur on the other side of the table as well. Your project leader may become so enraged at how stupid the user requests are that he or she will storm out of the room, leaving you just sitting there with your mouse in your hand. It's best to get ready for this in advance and think up an appropriate segue. Otherwise, just smile weakly and declare a 10-minute break.

The most interesting altercations occur between users. Procedural issues and questions of authority come out in any new development.

> *"Who's going to put the data in the system?"*
> *"Why I assumed Alice would do that."*
> *"Oh you did, did you? Well I don't take orders from you."*

Oh, boy. Unlike the characters in my brutal youth, people in a business environment don't beat each other senseless during an argument. Since this is a public forum, the users don't even get into full-bore screaming matches. After one of these encounters, the men involved grow grimly silent, offer no further discussion, and usually turn either ghostly white or beet red. Women narrow their eyes and shake a crossed leg like a metronome. The faster the speed, the greater their rage. There's nothing for you to do except sit there feeling awkward. After all, you just thought you were going to show how to press a command button to save data.

There will not be enough copies of any handout for all the people in the room. One of the developers will be asked to go make more. The desperate search for a photocopier that works will take 20 minutes. The resulting copies will be on the only available paper, which has holes for a three ring binder. These holes will obscure key text and encourage sharing of the original documents.

The cursor speed for the Windows mouse will be set to super-fast which will completely throw off the person trying to demo the system. "What the heck was that? Did you see that thing go? Where's the cursor now? Oh, there it is. Whoa, it won't stop! Get over there. Hey, you little @#%$." At this point, the users usually turn to each other with expressions conveying equal parts contempt, confirmation of the nerd status of the systems group, and the abandonment of any hope that the actual application will ever function properly.

Someone will remember a system he or she used that did just what your application does, only much better. It might have been an abandoned legacy system developed in-house or an off-the-shelf product. If this person is an old head developer he might be alluding to a system he worked on: "Let me tell ya, it was the greatest thing in the universe." "What you got here is a pale imitation. This thing was as fast as lightning. Heck, it could process a terabyte worth of data in a heartbeat, and make good strong coffee to boot. A little mechanical hand came out and stirred in the cream. Now that was a system. It was coded in good old SharkFace so it compiled down to nothing." Whatever this system was, any traces of it are completely gone. There are no copies, no manuals, no other people who can even vouch for its existence. Most likely, it ran in an entirely different platform and development environment. No matter, this ghost system will now become the yardstick by which your application will be judged.

This system will cast an intoxicating spell over everyone, especially if the initial storytelling is compelling. Soon all will crave it over your application. Some will even undergo hypnotherapy and remember during a life-regression that they too used the system and it was even better than Mr. Jeremy said it was. The users will chant, "Why can't your program work like the Phantom-2000?" at the start of any meeting. In all discussions from now on, you'll need to apologize that your system doesn't measure up to this mythical titan. This is perhaps the most hilarious thing that can happen in a user meeting. Just sit back and watch the madness.

The Application Life Cycle

Recruiters who call me on the phone always talk about how the proposed company is heavily into Application Life Cycle Development. Oooweee. Everyone in this industry loves jargon. I guess I'm supposed to get all steamed up about this. All I really want to know about is if there will be any women around who won't run away when they see me in the halls. As a programmer, the way a system is developed will, for the most part, be out of your hands. Your company might have Orwellian control over everything going on or you might have a hands-off supervisor who throws a rough spec on your desk and tells you to go ahead and use your best judgment. An Application Life Cycle is made up of phases that vary in number depending on how ambitious you are and what slick new book you just read. Here's an example along with my snide and less-than-enlightened comments.

Requirements Phase

This is the most user-intensive part of the process. Usually the chiefs sit down with the users and determine what it is they want the system to do. This can take an hour with a small system or an eternity in a large one. Requirements documents are written and then you try to get the users to sign them. This process takes longer than the requirements analysis itself. The development team wants users to sign in blood, they'd prefer to use the back of a spoon. You probably won't be involved in any of this process and might wonder why it is taking so long. This signing procedure is the dance of death for the users. Nobody wants to put his or her name on anything. After the documents are completed, the system moves into the design phase.

Design Phase

Once the requirements have been drawn up we move into the design phase. Here our goal is to create the skeleton that will later be covered with the flesh of our actual programming. If we want our monster to walk upright, we better get this phase done properly.

Physical Database Design

Design phase issues include determining the database structure. Tables, fields, and data relationships are defined. Key data fields and table indexes are established, and attempts are made to normalize to the nth degree. It's good to be vicious at this point about table design and relationships since the time of real data is still far away. Rewriting applications and moving data because of a database changes can be a brutal task. The more problems you solve while it's just up on the white board, the better. If you're allowed to participate in this part of the design, don't hold back any question you have. If a relationship isn't clear to you, then shout. Your input is useful because you're not exactly sure how it's suppose to operate. It's easy to miss a design flaw just because you're too close to it.

Data-Flow Diagrams

One method used to aid in database table design and overall system analysis is data-flow diagrams. There are a few different software packages and sleep-away camps devoted to this art form. The diagram attempts to model the flow of data through the system with a mix of bubbles, boxes, and arrows. The boxes represent data stores which are usually database tables. A book on the subject will point out that a data store could be almost anything, including a flat file or a shoe box. However, if your group is designing a system with a shoe box as a data store, you really ought to upgrade your server. The bubbles are the processes that the system performs, usually using data from one or more of the stores. The arrows show the data flow between the processes and the stores. A typical data model is bristling with these tiny spears, menacingly pointed at bubble and box alike.

I've been in several meetings during which data-flow diagrams were shown and, honestly, the only person who understood them was the one making the presentation. Drop one of these in the users' laps and you'd think you just poured hot coffee on them. The whole ordeal is made worse because the diagrams usually are shown with an overhead projector and transparencies. The lights are out, the projector's fan is pumping out heat and a steady drone, and the scent of the plastic transparencies mixes with the smell of the white board markers. The demonstrator is apparently immune, but everyone else is in a stunned, semi-hallucinatory state almost immediately.

Systems analysts love these bubble diagrams (Figure 7.1). As a programmer, I can't say I feel the same. The analysis is important but a bit too broad to help in coding. What I need to know is which tables my application needs and how they physically relate to each other. Can a certain field be blank? What fields are in the key? Which lookup tables do I need in the join? That's database design and sub module specs stuff.

Structured English Documents

For a brief time early in development, our group felt we needed to do structured English requirements documentation for all modules during the design phase. I found some of these the other day when I was moving out of my office. The intention was to write them so they are not in a programming language, or platform-specific so that you can just roll them up and tote them off to the beach, the movies, or the next development environment. The reasoning went something like this: "After these documents are written, then anyone, including nonprogrammers, can just refer to them and understand exactly what's going on in the system."

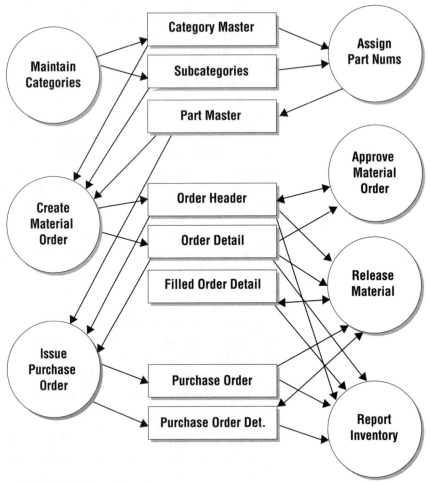

FIGURE 7.1 Data-flow diagram.

I am a programmer. I write code. I can't write English, structured or otherwise. You have ample evidence of that before you. No matter how we tried, we never wrote these things the way they wanted. They were revised three and four times and we never got any better at it. Such documentation isn't very helpful to a programmer. If there's a problem in the system, we go to the code, not some hack writing sample. I never understood who the intended audience really was, perhaps people who live in the bottom of a drawer, since that's where all our masterpieces ended up. If you have to do such writeups you have my sincerest sympathies. Find one that got a passing grade and crib what you can from it.

Sub Module Specifications Documents

One form of documentation that is useful to programmers is the sub module spec. Once the framework of the system is established, design might focus on functional decomposition. The system is broken down into bite-sized pieces that can later be distributed to the programmers. Specifications documents are written that usually explain what the module is, how it's supposed to function, and the database tables involved. Users are normally involved in this process, and there might be another mad dance to get the specs signed. Without written specs you can end up with a Sorta System (explained later on).

Flowcharts

One item you won't need in the design phase is your flowcharting template. Sure, you spent a whole month in computer school learning to use one of those things, but nobody's really going to sit there and do a flowchart. Someone might put one on the white board, but they'll use the wrong shapes for everything and your extensive training won't be of much help.

The one symbol on the flowcharting template that continues to captivate is the data drum. All systems analysts love that drum. At any opportunity they'll draw one on the board. Bring up vacation plans and they'll draw you a drum. Why do they like them? I guess it's a primal thing. Sometimes they go really wild and draw a drum with a lightning bolt shooting out of one side. I haven't been in a systems office yet that didn't have at least one drum sketched on the board.

Requirements and Design Summary

In no way do I wish to trivialize the importance of the requirements and design phases. They are vital to a successful application. If this analysis is done wrong, then your programming skills will be wasted. Development that rushes through these phases to get on with programming risks losing far more time later overhauling a poorly designed system. This is unfortunately the fate of a programmer. You are at the mercy of the system architects. If they screw up, it's you who'll pay the price. If you can get involved in the process, then do so. You might save yourself some future pain. Just don't snore during the data-flow model presentation or they won't ask you back for anything else.

Prototyping or Programming-Testing Phase

We now have a framework on which to begin actual programming. Programming is what I've been babbling about for most of this book, so here I'll keep it brief. You will be assigned one or more sub modules or programming tasks, and then you're on your own. I hope I have already convinced you of the benefits of adhering to standards in naming conventions, form design, and processing.

The Review Cycle

There may be one or more internal application reviews of your program within the development group, usually with the project leader and director. After this ordeal, there are several more reviews with the users. Programs that are simple or involve standard processing generally get through okay. Complicated processes don't fair as well. Required changes can be anything from easy screen layout fixes to major rewrites. If flaws in the system's design are discovered then the whole process might start over from the requirements phase. No matter what your program is, it's going to get overhauled. Expect this and brace yourself. Nothing gets through untouched. It was the result of doing countless revisions during this review cycle that I came to appreciate the techniques I have mentioned in this book.

Testing

Now that the programs are being developed, testing begins. I began my career as an applications tester. Testing applications is tedious, time-consuming, boring, and unbelievably important. Testers are in the unenviable position of having to tell people, over and over again, that what they are doing is wrong. Programmers see you and go pale. Then they argue. Then the filthy dogs just blame everything on the network. Having a person or department devoted full time to software quality assurance is a wonderful luxury that your company might not be able to afford. Without this, you'll have to rely on fellow programmers and the users.

In general programmers don't make very good testers. It is a different skill set and patience level. As I mentioned in the section in Chapter 3, "X-Ray Eyes," you become achingly familiar with your own program. You know how it's supposed to work so you don't even realize the ludicrous things the user will try to do. I wasn't a particularly good tester, but I was petty and vicious. This is the only way to get through an eight-hour day. That and caffeine. I drank five sodas a day when I was a tester.

A disciplined approach is necessary for proper testing. Ideally, it includes written test plans and plenty of time. When I tested, there were no plans. I did what is called keystroke or grunt-level testing. I just went in there and hacked around trying to break things.

Here is a rundown of some types of testing that your system may be put through:

★ **Unit Testing**: Testing that a single program works. Programmers are expected to unit test their own program to some degree, but we tend to be much kinder with our own work than a full-time tester. Take the time to create a small test plan that includes a checklist of items everyone should run through before claiming the program is finished.

★ **Integration Testing**: Testing that a group of programs or the entire system works as an interconnected unit. A bug in a key module may trickle down and adversely affect the entire system. Integration testing a large and highly interdependent application is very tricky and never finds everything. It's the degrees of freedom thing. There are so many ways you can go through the system that the number of permutations to test approaches infinity. That's an awful lot of sodas.

★ **Regression System**: Going back over the system to see if anything broke as a result of a changes to the system. You're trolling for new bugs. An old adage is that, for every five bugs fixed, one new bug is created. I guess that's an old adage. The guy who told me it was ancient.

★ **Multiuser Testing**: This is where concurrency and data integrity are put to the test. You don't actually need two people to do this, just two computers and a tester with long arms. Programs are tested to see what happens when users bump into each other, performing conflicting operations at the same time. Attempting to edit and save the same record is the real clincher. I did this testing for about a month in an old system, and there were so many problems that the whole project was scrapped.

★ **Beta Testing**: The system is put in the hands of the users toward the end of the test cycle. You might get one or two who'll really punch through the application, but don't expect most to be very enthusiastic about this task. Users get upset when they find bugs and generally don't remember what they were doing when it happened. This frustrates users and makes the developers crazy. Unclear bug fix requests usually end up in the "Could Not Duplicate" bin.

☆ **Acceptance Testing**: Performed by the users to determine if the system is acceptable and satisfies their requirements.

☆ **Final Validation Testing**: Performed by the users. Passing a final validation test doesn't mean the system doesn't have any bugs in it. It doesn't even mean the system is any good. I've seen some sinfully bad systems that survived final validation. It means that the system operated as they expected and the data that was entered was the data that came out. Your system did no harm. A final validation test might be mandatory depending on the industry and the type of the system. The company may need to provide documentation that a system passed a validation test in case of an inspection by authorities. The completed test plan is usually signed and stored in a vault guarded by wild apes.

Operation and Maintenance Phase

After surviving endless review cycles, user meetings, and testing runs, the system is finally ready for release as a version 1.0 system. If this system is replacing a legacy system, then the two may run in parallel for some time, perhaps three months or longer. During this time data is double-entered in both systems to make sure the new system is performing properly. This also allows you to slowly wean the users away from the old system. When the system runs with real users putting in real data, it's considered a live system. You have come to the end of a terrible journey. The system is in production. The system is alive. But we ain't done.

No matter how many steps you put in a Life Cycle, no one really pays attention until the system goes live, or until very late in development cycle. Then all hell breaks loose. It's sometimes hard to remember that the users aren't coming to work just to bask in the glory of your application. They've got other things to do with their time. To them, your application is a tool, like the scissors on their desks. We had a system that was released in prototype status for the users to play with. Maybe 30 people were given rights and told to go in and poke around. After six months I went in and looked at the log that tracked each time a user logged on to the system. Very few had bothered to go in even once. After all, this is just an in-house application, not a car wreck. What's to look at? It went live, somebody entered a record that they shouldn't have because they didn't understand the system, and screams of panic pierced the air.

If you think about it, the system really is meaningless to anyone until it starts running with real data. This is why the system always needs to be overhauled once it gets out there. This is going to happen every single time. If you let this part of the cycle get you upset, it will destroy you. I used to go insane when this happened. Didn't anybody even look at this? Wasn't anybody paying attention? A system in early stages of development is still just a dream. It hasn't forced itself into people's lives yet. Once the system is live, all the academic musings, network theories, and bubble charts that seemed so impressive get pushed naked and vulnerable into the real world. Some ideas are far less sturdy once they must get up off the page and actually perform.

Yes, there's definitely more to do after going live. Enhancements, bug fixes, and new sub modules are developed and added over the lifetime of the system. Small changes to the system usually occur piecemeal with executable files updated as necessary. More dramatic programming tasks might be considered a system release worthy of a new version number. Later versions usually include the cute stuff you didn't have time for in the system's brutal beginning. Regression testing now plays an increasingly important role. As a production system changes, you'll inevitably break a dish or two.

It is in this later maintenance and enhancement process that the coding standards become critical. You are looking at code written by other programmers or your own code written several years ago. Initial consistency and clarity in coding make the maintenance task a lot easier. I often have to go into projects I haven't touched in years. The standards, the constants, the Cradle to Grave variables, and the global routine calls are all in there. They have saved me an enormous amount of time maintaining a production system.

Project Management—Gantt Charts

The entire Life Cycle will probably be charted using a project management tool called a Gantt chart. There are several software packages devoted to creating these modern wonders. I've actually had to prepare these charts for people on two occasions using some of this software. There's a lot of jargon that goes along with Gantt charts, which makes managers love them all the more. Actually, the most interesting thing about them is that the moment they come out of the printer, they're out of date.

A Gantt chart isn't terribly sexy; it's just a piece of paper with a bunch of lines on it (Figure 7.2). Each line is a project task. Look

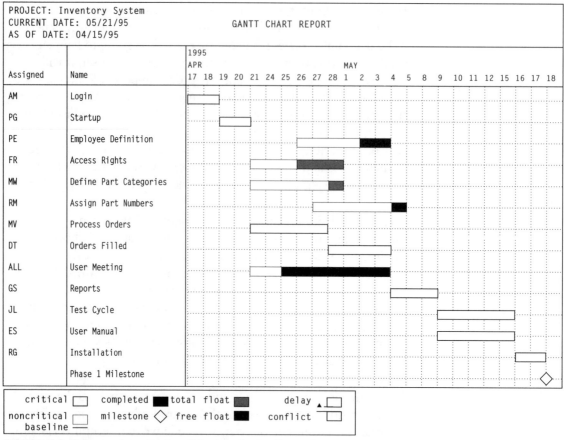

FIGURE 7.2 Printout from Project Schedule 5 of a Gantt chart.

for your initials, note your assignments, and ignore the rest. There's really only one thing that might be of interest. The critical path, perhaps better called anxiety road, are the tasks that must be completed in the time allotted or the project won't be finished on schedule. The other tasks can wait awhile. If you're on the critical path, you'll work like mad. If you're not, you slack around and generally annoy all the critty people.

One purpose of a Gantt chart is to give you something to hand out to executives when they wonder why the system is taking so long to develop. Pass them around in the meeting and the truth is told. They can't understand these things either. Just flip to the last page, shove your finger at the little diamond that signifies the final milestone and say, "We're actually way ahead of schedule."

For your own sake, learn how to read the time scale on these charts. I misinterpreted it on one and worked like a demon to finish something in the four days I thought were allotted. The project leader was shocked I finished so soon.

"You had 15 days to do that."

"The chart had four little blobs on it; wasn't that days?"

"You thought it was days? Who do you think you are, an executive?"

Whenever I get one of these charts now, I just take it and turn it face down on my desk.

It's difficult to estimate how long a programming task will take, especially if it's a brand new task and not a fix or enhancement to an existing project. When they prepare these charts, they really pump you for a time estimate. My advice is simple. You've already got the job, so don't bid low. Add extra time to your estimate. You'll look smart if you finish early, and you'll probably find you'll need more time than you thought anyway. I always evade the time question like I'm a car salesman ducking a price quote. "I dunno. I gotta look at it." That's my standard reply. It's a bit hard to graph.

Application Life Cycle Summary

You can probably tell by now that I don't consult for companies on Application Life Cycle development. I'm a a programmer, nothing more. There are plenty of stern books out there that will lay this all out a lot better than I just did. I felt it was necessary to include this section, benighted as it might be, since I've never seen a reference to any sort of development cycle in a standard programming manual. It's important to understand that the act of programming an in-house application is part of a much larger process.

I also don't want you to get the impression that I'm some lone nut developing applications for the family dog. I often feel this way when reading a programming manual. Have these authors ever dealt with a user? Have they ever had a system die in their arms? Have they ever needed to maintain a single line of code included in the companion diskette?

I can offer only this advice. At all times listen to the users. They aren't idiots. The development group members are not geniuses. You don't know what's best for users. You can't force a system down their throats. If you make this crucial mistake, then the system is doomed. If the lowliest user says the design won't work for whatever reason, then you better listen. Involve users in as much of the process as possible. Don't think you're going to go underground, do a skunkworks project, then show it to the users and win a glorious victory. You must ask, continue to ask, and demand an answer to the following questions:

1. Are the assumptions currently built in to the design reasonable? Will this system work here, now, and in a way that you are comfortable with?
2. Does this system make sense to you?
3. Is this system's operation unlike what is currently in place? If so, are you comfortable with this difference? What could happen that would invalidate the design? Is this likely? What will we do if it happens?
4. Are you confused? Why? What can be made clearer?

If at all possible, get your hands on real data (historical or otherwise) that can be used in the system throughout the development cycle instead of making up gobbledygook. Meaningless test data doesn't help matters. "Here's a report that's lists summary totals of guzzleheads sorted by budgpukums. You can see how nicely it lines up the decimal points." A lot of effort went into that report, but no one cares. If the users are presented with sensible data, they are more likely to understand what the system is doing and get involved in process. You'll also flag problems that would have otherwise gone unnoticed in a dippy data set.

If you are replacing a system currently in use, find out how that system works and what the users like about it. It might be junk, but the users have grown accustomed to its idiosyncrasies and are comfortable working with it. Now you're coming in, a collective fresh-faced development kid, with a system they might not want to use. If this old system is DOS-based, then wipe that smirk off your face. The horrible truth is that all this fancy Windows stuff doesn't impress users. If they like that old system, you're in for a long fight. Users can really crank in some of those old DOS systems. I can still go into some old programs I haven't used in years and plow through on muscle memory alone. I'm hitting **F5** to save, **Alt-Z** to copy, **Shift-Tab** to view, and I don't even remember why. The users will suddenly need to upgrade the sad 286s they're using now and need Windows training. Your application will still run slower than old DOS lightning, and they'll wonder what all the fuss was about.

The most horrible thing that can happen is that the users hate the system. Often they aren't even specific as to why. It's just a raw hate. This should be addressed at once and should be considered an absolute priority. If you ignore this, it won't go away. Don't think, "Tough, they better get used to it." You need to stop and find out exactly what it is that's sending them into a rage. Don't settle for a general grumbling. If you get the absolute specifics, you might find that the changes required to make the users happy take just a few hours. If you keep plowing ahead, you'll end up with a system no one will use.

Listening to users spit out venomous comments about a system you're pouring your soul into is about the worst experience you can have. You must (and, honestly, I sometimes can't do this) accept that they are telling the truth. Remember they are angry because your system is causing them pain. If you address the problem immediately, you have a chance of saving the system.

Finally, when discussing anything with users do not stand with your arms folded in front of you. If they are sitting, then you should sit. If there is no chair, then crouch on the floor. Do not lord over the user. They can and will make your life miserable if you treat them with contempt. You exist only if you make their lives easier. Your system exists only if it serves their interests. If you start thinking of the development group and the users as Us vs. Them, you're never going to make it.

The Sorta System

I would now like to offer you my own simple, one-phase application Life Cycle. It is actually used in many companies, especially by small and new development groups. It is known as the Sorta System. Someone sorta explains what they want the system to do. You sorta understand what they said and start developing. The system sorta works the way you thought it should. In the user demo, they don't like it and sorta explain what needs to be changed. You again sorta understand and rewrite it. Eventually, a system is sorta developed and it does sorta work. Sometimes. This can be a wonderful thousand-year Life Cycle as development slowly inches forward, then takes a step back, then forth, then side to side, and around again.

The Sorta System is popular because people are comfortable thinking in this way. Sorta is fine in most situations. "Just put it down over there some place." *Thunk.* "Good enough." It is not fine in a computer system. Imagine this exchange between a person and a building contractor:

> *"Go build me a house."*
> *"What kind of house?"*
> *"Why, a nice one, of course."*

Is there any way this person is going to be happy when the house is finished? This stuff happens to me all the time. Now that it's built, the whole house needs to be uprooted and moved back 10 feet to make room for a sunporch.

People seem to find the Sorta System idea amusing so you can use it to your advantage in development. It's actually fun to shout this at a meeting. "If you don't tell me what you want then this is going to be another lousy Sorta System!" This can actually salvage a meeting gone awry. I'd rather have everyone chant this and get back on track than settle for vague and half-hearted requirements.

The Sorta System methodology results from a lack of specific requirements. Large firms have the opposite problem. The amount of paper that must be generated chokes development. Programmers spend more time updating system documentation than actually coding. The paperwork that must accompany a programming change can take longer to do than the actual fix itself. Your system can become mired in bureaucracy and politics.

If you hire a consulting company to manage your application Life Cycle, they'll have you pushing so much paper, you'll probably never get around to real coding ever again. I guess it's either spew or stew. You spew out paper that grinds development to a halt, or you stew at the end of development rewriting misguided prototypes. This will be completely out of your hands. It's something to ask about in the interview. Act innocent and you might get an honest answer. (Spew or stew? I've finally lost it.)

Chutes and Ladders

There is no way to predict what will happen to your application as it travels through its intended Life Cycle. Here are a few case studies of the many unexpected paths a system can take.

★ Case 1: The original system is very simple and designed for one user. Tentatively, it's given to another user, then another. Slowly, requests for additional modules and enhancements come in. The system grows into a huge project far beyond its humble beginnings.

★ Case 2: The original system is grandiose in design and scope. Enormous effort is put into creating a fully integrated application that culls data from everywhere and everybody. The users are pushing for this Big Brother system all the way throughout development. Then they realize the time and effort needed to maintain the system and begin to gripe. No one is willing to go through the trouble to use the entire system, and pieces are slowly discarded. Eventually, the system is little more than a shell of its former self. The users who initially cringed at the sight of the large system now fall in love with this little nub, while acres of code lay fallow in an archive directory.

★ Case 3: An enormous project is undertaken and worked on for years. At the tail end of development, a fatal flaw will be found in the system. This is usually an error in database design or a severe overall programming problem like a lack of multiuser capability. The time and effort to fix the system will be so great that it will just be abandoned. It ends up one of the dead hulks mentioned in the next section "Legacy Systems."

★ Case 4: A system is originally designed in a generic fashion so that it can be used in many situations. As development continues, it becomes custom-tailored to a specific user or workgroup. This person or group does things like nobody else in the world. Even the programmers laugh at the changes that are being made. Finally, the system fits the twisted vision of this particular user community. The interested parties then depart from the company and the poor thing just sits idle, now far too weird for anyone else to play with.

★ Case 5: A system is reworked so much over time that it's original intentions are barely recognizable. The code has become so convoluted with patches and workarounds that all programmers pray they won't be called in to do anything. The system will be unbelievably vital to the company so it can't be abandoned. Some poor soul might spend his or her whole life just trying to maintain this system.

☆ Case 6: A special system is developed by an individual who everyone believes to be a programming genius. This person then leaves and someone else must take over the system. After reviewing the code, the maintenance programmer returns to the project leader shuddering with fear.
"What's wrong?"
"The code."
"The code?"
"The code. I have no idea what Allen was doing. I mean, don't get me wrong, the system's working . . ."
"So what's the problem?"
"I have no idea why. He just did things in there that you wouldn't believe."

No one else will be able to decipher this awful program either. It will be entirely rewritten from scratch, and the original version will be defused and dismantled by the bomb squad.

Legacy Systems: A Dynasty of Code

Legacy System. Real cool name. A legacy system is a wretched old program that's probably been kicking around since COBOL was the hip language. Actually, it might have been written in COBOL. Although you hope to work on new Windows development using

Visual Basic and client/server, your company might have other plans. Be wary, if on your first day of work, you're introduced as the new entry-level programmer with a VB background (a one-week course), and everyone in the development group seems overly delighted to meet you. It's probably because you're going to be given the awful task of maintaining some dying ember of a system while they now get to work on the fun stuff since a fresh kitchen knave has been found.

Ask about the programming mix in the interview. Find out how much time is spent on developing and maintaining shiny new systems and how much is spent trying to prop up tired old plowhorse applications. Determine where you'll fit in this scheme. Do you get to brave new trails or are you stuck in the cellar? If you're being hired because you still know some dead language, then your fate is sealed. It's legacy. The interviewer will assure you that you'll get to work on new development too, but there's no guarantee. It's sad seeing this happen. A programmer is hired, eager to dive into Windows programming, just as soon as he or she finishes fixing a coding assignment in an old system. "Once this is done, I can join the rest of you." Oh, you could just cry. Legacy work is never done. It's a legacy because it's still vital to the company's well-being. You'll be haunting that creaky old mansion for years to come.

Maintaining a legacy has been referred to as system archeology. If you think you've seen bad code, wait until you get a look at these babies. There are usually convoluted workarounds used because certain commands or functions just didn't exist. Standards and naming conventions will be nonexistent. If documentation exists, it will be written by someone who obviously didn't think anyone would actually read it. Be careful. Comment every section of code you write, including your name and the date. You'll need to determine friend or foe as you go through this thing. Try to find someone who can tell you something about the development history, including the cast of characters. This person will probably be thrilled to tell you about it. I relish retelling tall tales about systems past.

As with all programming tasks, once you touch that code, it's yours. Don't volunteer to go poking around making changes in one of these things. Suddenly, every problem that happens in the system will become your responsibility. Sit on your hands when they ask for volunteers to go spelunking through the code. There are no hidden treasures to be found, trust me.

Some legacy systems have a wonderful maintenance-free quality. There's no source code. Where is it? Nobody knows. Nothing but compiled files ready to run. This charmer probably worked for years and nobody noticed the cupboard was bare. Now that there are programming changes needed, there's nothing that can be done. The system is dead. Sure some nut could probably buy a decompiler and convert it to assembler, but who's touching that code? I had the pleasure of discovering one of these code-free systems. It's fun trying to explain the predicament to an assembled group of bigwigs since it's a real big mistake and I didn't make it. Who's watching the store, guys? Sometimes life is kind.

You will eventually come across a small group of users who have managed to create their own cargo cult around an application that nobody knew existed or didn't realize anybody used anymore. No one can remember where this software came from or who wrote it, but this group clings to it for their very survival. You'll hear about it when someone calls the help desk and requests a bug fix or enhancement. It is quite a spooky experience.

Another weird experience is coming across the dead hulk of an abandoned legacy system lying in a holding bin somewhere. The source code is just rotting away on an unused server volume. You scroll through the system's employee table, but see no recognizable names. You might find a whole room filled with old meeting notes, user manuals and documentation. Cartons are filled with pamphlets promising great things just around the corner, and a trade show booth is packed up tight. There's a bottle of champagne to celebrate an occasion that never came. It's like seeing a family photo album in a garbage can. Someone threw a life away, but you don't know why.

Freshman Lexicon

As a service to anyone just getting out of school, here's a brief rundown of people and phrases you're going to encounter once you get past the smiling interviewer and start your career as a Data Processing Professional.

Executive Wing

As you move up in the corporation, your duties become increasing less definable. Eventually, they become so nebulous it's almost impossible to determine if you're actually doing your job. At this point you move into the executive wing. This is where the company keeps its upper managers so they don't have to mix with the general population. Accidentally wandering into this rarefied sanctum is usually an eye-opening experience. I had to venture in there during my help desk days. The carpeting is about an inch thick and the rubber trees are actually watered on a regular basis. Unlike the battered metal and ramshackle fiberboard trappings of the rest of the organization, executive furniture is made of finely crafted wood. It gives off a wonderful cherry glow, perfectly matching the hue of the attending secretary's hair. An executive's secretary is usually so ridiculously beautiful she seems to be an image out of a dream state. You'll be ushered out of here quickly before someone spots you and calls security.

CEO or Chief Executive Officer

The big boss. If you're wondering why CEOs make so much money, I can summarize it in two words: vague pleasantness. CEOs are carefully trained at executive commando school to speak in hushed grandfatherly tones at all public functions, thereby nullifying any discord. New CEOs really shine when they make a speech introducing themselves to the employees.

> *"I'd just like to remind you all of one thing.*
> *The past is behind us.*
> *The future is ahead of us.*
> *The present is right now.*
> *Thank you very much."*

Read the letter to the stockholders in your company's annual report for more examples. Pick one from when the stock price crashed from $97 to $3. Take heart dear friends, we're in a transitional year.

While he may be a master of vague pleasantness, don't make the mistake of showing a new CEO around the shop as if he was actually interested in how many file servers you have. He didn't get in his current position by humoring people in the systems department. If you persist in engaging a CEO in a technical discussion, watch him glare at you like you're an alley cat offering him the dead weasel in your mouth.

CIO or Chief Information Officer

The CIO is in a rather precarious position. For the most part, no one is really quite sure what the CIO is supposed to do. He is a three-letter executive and is thus expected to devote much of the day to pleasantries. Yet this person must also act as commander of all the company's information technology. If he is too technical, he loses the respect of the other executives who expect the CIO to fit the upper management mold of bold hand gestures and timid five-year plans. If the CIO was really technically inclined he would have never made it this far, but if he knows nothing at all he loses the respect of the people he's overseeing. It's not easy being the king. As a result, CIOs usually don't last too long. They get cut loose after about a year and drift off to some other executive playground.

As with all executives, on the CIO's desk there will usually be an obelisk, a brass eagle with outstretched wings, or a letter opener in the shape of a cavalry sword. In addition, the computer will be installed with an enormous collection of jaunty screen savers which are needed to prevent the ravages of phosphor burn-in. On the white board will be a solitary data drum, unnamed and unconnected to any systems project, drawn primarily out of *esprit de corps*.

The CIO won't give you a dirty look if you start talking tech, but most likely will have no idea what you're saying. Some malicious employees create nonexistent technical terms and include them in such discussions. Remember, CIOs have also attended executive commando school and know that no matter what is said they should just to nod and smile. If you have just been promoted to a CIO position, remember the following phrase and you should do just fine, "That's a good idea. We should look into that." Vague and pleasant. Very nice.

Management Books

Wonderfully unreadable nonsense about synergy, empowerment, and mission-oriented action steps. Presumably read by the executives in an attempt to stay current. Someone in our company sends out an e-mail with a snippet from one of these books every day. No one has a clue what the paragraph is saying. I've actually deconstructed a few word by word and still have no idea. These books succeed in making topics of general interest as ponderous and obscure as a Hegel rant.

Occasionally they dumb it all down to an acronym like the following:
 "Peak performers rely on TRUST:
 ***T** eamwork,*
 ***R** esponsibility,*

U nderstanding,
S trategy, and
T owel Snapping"

Several hundred pages are then devoted to each of the letters. I can't imagine putting much faith in a philosophy with tenets concocted to spell out a nifty buzzword.

Programmer, Junior Level

Originally called entry-level programmers, but since every 16-year-old working in the mall is considered an assistant manager, the title was upgraded. I was a junior programmer for a good long while. Unfortunately, as a junior, you get tossed the bare coding bones after the senior programmers have picked the application carcass clean of the interesting assignments. If you're really unlucky, you spend your junior days doing things like formatting floppy disks and dreaming of better times ahead. The first thing new junior programmers do is meet someone on staff they consider a genius. Later on they'll inherit one of this person's applications and realize what a folly that was.

Programmer, Senior Level

A seasoned programmer covered with scars and filled with war stories. Gets first pick of programming assignments. May help the systems analyst in design-related issues. Usually doesn't get dressed up for work even if the company requires it. Knows they won't fire him or her since the amount of time and effort to train another person to understand the company's applications far outweighs requiring formal attire.

Applications Tester

Besides one's primary duties, which are to ensure the overall quality of application development, there is a special skill a tester needs that won't be in the job description. As a tester you must master the almost impossible task of telling programmers they've screwed up royally without damaging their egos (which can be considerable) or igniting their ire. While most of the organization might take the quality of their work cavalierly, programmers never do. Programming is a very personal, oddly creative art. Telling a programmer that they write bad code is an insult that really can't be translated into civilian terms.

Project Leader

Orchestrates the activities of many programmers working on an application. Must make the awful decision of who gets the plum assignments and who gets the duds. Also acts as a buffer between the users and the development community. Must be able to translate a user's helplessly turbid request into an actual programming assignment.

Systems Analyst, Senior

Responsible for establishing the framework of an application, including such decisions as what platform and programming language, database design, and general development direction. A systems analyst's office is usually lined with bookshelves filled with shiny manuals. In mass quantities, this creates the illusion of lacquered walls.

Aging systems analysts love to tell stories about the bad old days when they had to load the operating system from a paper feed and kick the Burroughs machine to get it to run. Don't roll your eyes during these stories or they'll have you formatting floppies with the junior league.

Occasionally, a systems analyst will show his or her true colors and announce something ridiculous like, "After my in-depth analysis, the programming will be trivial." After the programmers get wind of such a pronouncement, they burn this person in effigy at a secret ceremony.

(Also Syssy Boys, Drum Lovers)

Hardware Specialist

The only job in the systems department that has any macho overtones. The old hardware specialist at our company could convincingly describe the act of turning on a computer as "firing it up." The office is usually strewn with the scavenged remains and half-eaten husks of the company's computers, possibly to the point that it hampers mobility. Hardware specialists occasionally get to crawl around under the executive secretary's desk, propelling the programmers into fits of jealous rage.

Programmer Wannabees

Oddly enough, some people actually look up to programmers and wish they were one too. This is impossible for most people to believe.

There certainly aren't any middle management Wannabes anymore. "Ooh, some day I'll have metal furniture and a rolodex. Then everyone will have to respect me. I'll date nothing but leggy supermodels."

Absolute contempt is heaped upon programmer wannabes. I guess I was considered one back when I was a tester. When I'd ask the programmers a coding question, they'd inevitably break out in a nasty smile. I could read their minds, "Who's this idiot think he is? Go back to your cube little boy. Let the real men worry about the programming." The contempt is far greater if it's a manager spouting off some ridiculous idea he read in a computer magazine. Critical mass is reached if the manager also wears red suspenders and/or fancy socks.

Groupies

There are no programmer groupies. I've checked.

Users

Employees who actually use your in-house application. It has been argued that they should be called something else, like clients, but that's never caught on. The term user in itself is not derogatory unless prefixed with the word stupid, which is often the case. Programmers occasionally engage in discussions during which they ponder what on earth the users actually do with their time. For better or worse, there's nothing vague about programming. At the end of the day you know exactly what you've accomplished. You wrote this, you fixed that, you can even count all the lines of code if you want. But what about facilitators, coordinators, planners, and all the other pretty people? The titles sure sound nice, but do they actually do anything?

I'm Not Technical

Phrase spoken by users when someone in the systems group asks them any computer-related question. Said roughly in the same tone as someone would say, "I'm not an axe-murderer."

Cut a Check

What you have to get the Finance department to do before you can order that new file server. Everyone in the organization loves to say this (again, the reason escapes me) and will do so at any given opportunity.

Pocket Protector

What all the computer-illiterate people in the organization will claim that everyone in the systems group has. A more appropriate observation might be an oversized coffee mug with a slogan like "CyberAnaGenuflect—Tomorrow's Technology Today." A souvenir hard won by sitting through a 20-minute vendor demo at a Comdex Conference.

Nemesis

All programmers have one program or system they absolutely loathe, but it never goes away. The users love it, the company adores it, and everybody wants changes and enhancements. All you want to do is bury the whole thing in the backyard. Just when you think you've finally heard the last of it, more calls will come in for extra reports, twisted logic changes, and other assorted demands.

Bear

Extremely difficult programming assignment.

Bio-Break

Five-minute break in a long user meeting so everyone can deal with the inevitable effects of three cups of coffee.

Nontrivial

Same as Bear.

Dog and Pony Show

A formal demo of an application, usually involving handouts, overheads, and starched white shirts.

Smoke and Mirrors

An over-hyped application that doesn't perform as advertised. This can include a jury-rigged demo version of a system. It gives the impression of functionality that doesn't exist or doesn't work properly once you stray off the guided tour. If your salesperson has got a firm chin and a whiskey baritone you can sell a totally nonexistent system using transparencies and glossy brochures alone. Clients who have been sold smoke and mirrors instead of a functional application get very angry, very quickly.

(Also VaporWare)

Bit-Fiddling Geek

Big deal, hot-shot programmer who probably codes in assembly and/or C++. I'm guessing the term is derogatory. I've never actually heard someone say this in-house.

(also Bit-Twiddling Geek, Propeller Head, Dork Raised to the Nth Power)

Cowboy

Programmer, typically a consultant, who comes in, makes a programming mess, then leaves.

Body Shop

Computer consulting firm. As a result of company cutbacks, computer consulting firms do a thriving business. Companies would rather have a consultant come in for a few weeks than support a full-time development staff. Some consulting firms treat their employees fairly, others live up to the nickname. Find out before you sign on. Go ahead and ask it outright in the interview just to shake them up, "Is this a Body Shop? No? Why not?" Don't worry, they won't throw you out. These places need Windows programmers in the worst way.

Beach

Where you end up in a Body Shop between programming contracts. Depending on your skill set, a day on the beach can turn into a month without pay.

Technical Recruiter

Person who works for a Body Shop trying to get programmers after the company has bid a contract. Generally despised by programmers. I completely unnerved a recruiter by asking about programming standards. He said the company didn't have any. I went into a long rant about how bad that was and he actually starting trembling. Then he told me he wasn't technical. I kept at him anyway, occasionally leaning back in my chair smirking like Mickey Rourke, as he stammered though his replies. I kept waiting for him to jump out the window (also **Head Hunter**).

Technical Job Fair

A job fair focused on computers and related occupations. Some have nothing but Body Shops in attendance. The fair might rent out an entire floor of a fancy hotel. All the smiling recruiters stalk the hallways, preying upon the unwary. When I go to one of the Body Shop Job Fairs just for fun, I don't wear a suit jacket and literally frighten everyone. The whole herd of Data Processing Professionals is glumly slumping along, encased in the required blue armor. I'm there in a blinding white shirt. "Is he crazy? Doesn't he know you must look professional to get hired by a good company?" Hey, I'm a Windows programmer. I'll wear whatever I want. Try this stunt only if you're already gainfully employed.

The same trick works in a standard job interview. The truth is, the purpose of the business suit is to distinguish people in the building who aren't real employees. No one keeps their suit jacket on throughout the day. It's hung behind the door as soon as you come in. Anyone wearing a jacket is either a salesperson, a vendor, or a sad-sack on an interview. By not wearing one, you destroy this whole scheme. Again, please don't do this if you really need the job. It's just that unnerving people in interviews is a pastime of mine. (My failed attempt to try to get out more.)

401K

Benefit that's supposed to justify why you make half the salary of someone in a Body Shop.

Bare Midriffs

What executives fear will result if they decide to establish a "dress-down Friday." An explicit prohibition is usually included with the announcement of such a policy. For older executives, dress-down day confirms their belief that society is about to collapse. Some may attempt to get into the spirit and actually wear jeans like everyone else. However, theirs are distinguished by a front crease pressed in as deeply as an officer's uniform.

Beige Cubicles

Where executives plop down the rest of the organization. If set up in large numbers, they actually affect one's depth perception, making it difficult to navigate outside one's immediate environs. This is probably an intended side effect. No matter what the acoustic rating of a cubicle, spicy phone conversations can be heard by all adjoining staff no matter how low the person attempts to speak. Such cubicles are called panel systems in the office supply trade. Beige is known as Harvest Wheat.

Phosphor Burn-In

What your screen saver is supposed to prevent.

Fortune 500 Company

Where recruiters brag that they can get you a job. You're supposed to jump up and down rejoicing, and forget that many of these companies are still using COBOL and RPG III for most of their programming tasks.

800 Years Experience

Companies often like to pump up their image by stating how much experience their staff has. Sometimes they carry this to a hilarious extreme by quoting the sum of all the employee's experience instead of the average, as if someone in the company was actually writing programs in the twelfth century. My old firm actually did this in ads seen by thousands, and I had to laugh every time I saw one.

Applications Developer

What programmers tell someone they do for a living when asked at a wedding and other social functions. Necessary because if you say, "I'm a computer programmer," people make a face and run away. I learned this one the hard way. Your best bet: "I work indoors."

Data Processing Professionals

The euphemism that large newspaper ads use when looking for programmers and other systems people.

A Very Prestigious Company

Where young, newly hired employees tell people that they work. No one who's been in any company longer than a year still considers it prestigious. You often see this in ads for computer training schools. "I'm so happy, I just got a great job at a very prestigious company!" Just wait, junior. Just wait.

Satisfaction in a Job Well Done

What your boss will tell you that you have instead of the raise you just asked for.

It Is Finished

You've just read everything I learned the hard way about Visual Basic/SQL applications development. I've tried to be entertaining and I've tried to be honest. It has not been easy. My friend who did the illustrations for this book asked me why on earth I kept on writing when it was apparent to everyone that it was sending me over the edge. "A computer manual? Who reads those things?" he said. "I saw a whole bin of them in the bookstore, and they were all marked down to a dollar."

The truth is, I didn't write this to have fun. I didn't write this to make money. I wrote it because it's everything I know and thought it might be useful to someone. It is—and this is a really horrible thought—my life story. If people like it, I'll be elated; if people hate it, I'll be miserable. Either way, it'll end up in the discount bin. As always, I will be at the computer, pounding the keyboard, my head, the desk, and whatever else comes in handy. Women will still avoid me in the halls.

You certainly don't have to use or agree with my suggestions and techniques. I just hope you understand the purpose behind them and think about them when designing your own projects. The purpose of naming conventions, global routines/forms, a template project, and standardized processing is the same. They are designed to reduce friction during setup, programming, and maintenance of a system. You don't stumble over variables wondering about their type or scope. You don't waste time creating and setting up a new form. Much of the boring, drudge coding is replaced by a call to a generic routine or form. Projects can be added to and maintained by a series of people without chaos. You can focus your attention on the important core logic, the bug fix, or the enhancement instead of constantly looking down so you don't trip over your untied coding laces.

I've worked in systems both with and without standards. The time saved throwing that application together without them is eaten up later on in excessive maintenance time, obscure bugs, and rewrites. If you do nothing but take a few minutes to establish some standards of your own, I'll die a happy man.

I just hope nothing I've written has persuaded anyone to become a programmer. My intentions were the opposite. Computer programming is not easy. It is often absolutely agonizing. It would be a disservice for me to tell you otherwise. If you haven't yet taken the plunge into serious applications programming, you should ask yourself why you really want to do something so torturous for a living. If you really have an option, then leave the programming to feral wolf boys like me. I'll end with a story that perhaps can help you decide.

I remember attending an assembly when I was in elementary school. The featured performer was Mr. Jiggs, a chimpanzee. Mr. Jiggs was a cute little thing dressed in overalls and a bright red shirt. He could make faces on command and perform simple tricks. The trainer also pointed out that since Mr. Jiggs was a chimpanzee he was strong enough to rip a man's arms off. Mr. Jiggs was then outfitted with roller-skates and was let loose to whiz around an auditorium filled with children. Before he was released, the trainer made a grave announcement. "DO NOT TOUCH HIM. I REPEAT: DO NOT TOUCH HIM." Mr. Jiggs then sped off the stage, and every single kid stiffened up, petrified with fear.

I happened to be sitting in the end seat of the last row in the auditorium, and here's this crazed monkey barreling down the aisle. All I can think is that he's going to misjudge the turn, slam into me, and then rip my arms off. When I leave for home at the end of the day, the teacher will wrap my limbs around my neck like a sweater and I'll have to carry my lunch box in my teeth. Then my mom will demand a reason why my arms have been ripped off. I'll have to convince her that it wasn't my fault; it was a monkey at school dressed like Farmer Brown.

Mr. Jiggs flew past me. He turned wide and I remained safe and undismembered. It was one of the oddest, happiest moments of my life. I sat there grinning like a fool, just like all the other aisle kids. I'd finally achieved something. I'd actually survived an encounter with a chimpanzee on roller-skates.

This is why you become a programmer. It isn't that "computers are the wave of the future" or some other garbage. You see, when you're a programmer, you sit in that end seat of the last row every single day. Most of the time, that stupid, angry monkey misjudges the turn and you're left with bloody stumps where your arms should be.

But once in a great while, that little guy puts on those skates and he zooms right past, and you'd swear he was looking at you with a big smile on his face. For just a brief moment, you can't help but think that this is the coolest thing you've ever seen. And you feel kind of sorry for all those kids sitting in the safety of the middle seats. They're really missing a great show.

INDEX